Voices fror
AN ENGLISH
VILLAGE

Cheddington

Memories of
The Second World War

Compiled and Edited by Jane Cutler, with assistance from

Jean Fulton, John T Smith and Denise Webb

Cheddington History Society

Cheddington History Society

Cover illustration by Meg Grant

Cover design by Behram Kapadia

ISBN: 978-0-9567483-0-0

The Cheddington History Society thanks the Cheddington Parish Council and the Buckinghamshire County Council Community Leaders' Fund for their grants towards the cost of this publication.

Printed by Parchments of Oxford
Printworks, Crescent Road, Cowley, Oxford, England, OX4 2PB
email: print@parchmentuk.com   www.PrintUK.com

Foreword

In May 2005, at the suggestion of Marlene Lee, our archivist, the Cheddington History Society held an exhibition to commemorate the 60th anniversary of VE Day. It was more successful than we imagined. Visitors came from neighbouring towns and villages and we even had one gentleman from Wisconsin, USA who was on holiday in Tring. We decided that, during the exhibition, it would be a good opportunity to collect memories of VE Day. Some of the war stories were fascinating and we followed them up in people's homes. In the intervening years the collection of memories grew and we felt that we should publish them so that we could share our new appreciation of the Second World War with others. Sometimes people's memories of the same event may differ.

Jane Cutler

When I took over the Cheddington History Society Archives in 2004, I was very taken with the photographs of men and women from the village who had served in World War II. I knew that many were no longer with us but still had wives and relatives living here. The 60th anniversary of VE Day was just around the corner (May 2005) and I thought what a good opportunity it would be to honour these people and to tell their story to a new generation.

My own memories of the war are still very vivid and I wanted to tell today's school children what it was like to be a child then - and so the idea of holding an exhibition was born and gradually took root. I was delighted that so many children came and showed such an interest. One lovely memory I have of the exhibition is of a little girl who, on being told how I had slept for many weeks under the stairs, replied "Oooh – just like Harry Potter." Fame indeed.

Marlene Lee, July 2010

CONTENTS I

CONTENTS II

FATHER WAS A STRANGER WHEN HE RETURNED FROM WAR

I was born during the war, in Cheltenham. My father had joined the RAF and, after training at places like Beer and Tenby, he served in North Africa and Italy in radar. My earliest memory of him is when I opened the door to someone who was a complete stranger, when he returned from the war.

Cheddington High Street, the School with the clock tower (undated)

Village Green & Memorial, Cheddington, Bucks.

Cheddington Village Green and War Memorial Note the Old Inn sign on right where the pub used to be (undated)

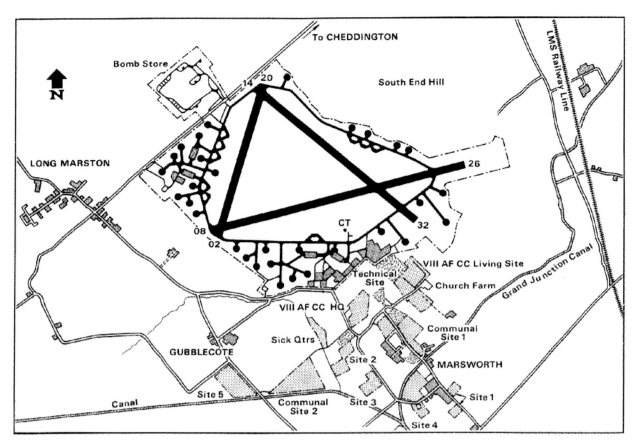

Cheddington Airfield in the Second World War

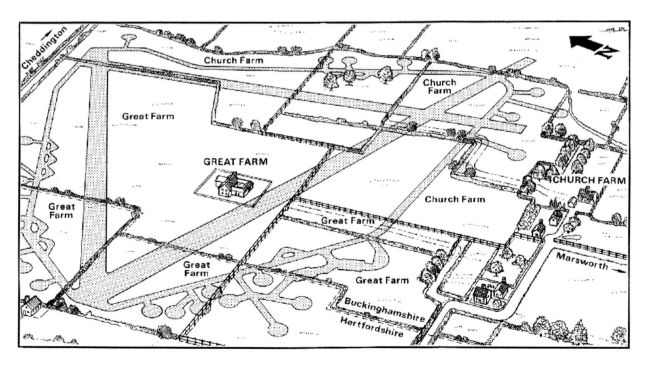

Cheddington Airfield on land at Church Farm

Ivan Janes

See map on inside front cover for location of sites mentioned in Ivan's memories.

BORN IN CHEDDINGTON

I was born in one of the cottages at South End opposite The Swan in 1927. Then we moved to 12 Manor Road (this was first called Westend) into a new house in 1936 and so when the war started in 1939 I was living there. I was only a young lad at the outbreak of war and there was not much to do in the village.

ISSUING OF GAS MASKS

They issued us with gas masks in the chapel on the village green. Then we had to go through this van parked by the bus stop to test them. It made you feel sick from the rubbery smell on the gas mask. The service gas masks (the Army) were different from ours. They had a long tube down to the filter and the straps went round the waist. We just had a filter where the mask fitted onto your face.

THE EVACUEES

The evacuees came after the issuing of gas masks. When they turned up someone on a committee came round to each house to check if there was room for an evacuee. We didn't have one because there were a lot of us in the family. There were seven of us in a three bedroom house. People had to have the evacuees whether they wanted them or not. Through them being extra, the school wasn't big enough. They used the church hall as a school (this is now the scout hut), the Wesleyan Chapel room at the back, and the Old Reading Room was used as a school as well.

We all got on with them well. A lot of them were Londoners and we all mixed well. A lot of evacuees lived in Andrews Terrace, the Dunns, the Hillyards, and the Lyons families. There were about 10 two bed cottages. There were also evacuees at the big house with bow windows near The Green, this house was divided into two. The houses in Andrews Terrace were condemned cottages. They were damp and had black beetles and outside toilets.

SHOPS IN CHEDDINGTON

There were three shops in Cheddington during the war years, Mrs Turner at The Green, Tappy May's in New Street, and Mr Mason's on the High Street. People living in the village used to get their Rations which were allowed from them. We also had a Baker's shop where Christmas Cottage is now.

Tappy May's shop at the end of Andrews Terrace sold all sorts of stuff. Not vegetables, you didn't see many vegetables that time of day, people grew them in gardens. She used to sell paraffin oil at the back of the shop. When you undid the shop door a little bell used to ring on top of the door. You might have to wait two or three minutes. And when she came she would check your pockets to see if you had put any sweets in. She done that with everybody.

There was three coal merchants in the village, Mr Fathers, Mr Boarder and Labrums. We were only allowed 1 cwt (hundred weight) which didn't warm us much, so we all relied on finding wood to burn to keep us warm and for cooking we only had little cooking ranges for use, there was no central heating them days, you had to keep warm with overcoats on.

WORKING WITH THE PHEASANTS ON THE LINCES

In the evenings and weekends I used to go down Bishop's Farm with Mr Bishop's sons doing odd jobs to earn sixpence. There was one son, Sailor Bishop (George) who used to be in the Navy. He was on the Royal Naval Reserve and three days after war was declared he was called up. And up till then he had all these pheasants on top of the Linces (facing the canal) and I used to help him with the pheasants. We had two shepherd's huts, one on top of the hill that we used to sleep in to guard the pheasants, and the other hut was to keep the food stuff for pheasants. The hens looked after the pheasant's eggs in coops. The hen was ringed on the leg with a cord attached, one yard, so it couldn't get away. The water used to be outside for it to drink. When the pheasant's eggs were hatched I used to collect the eggs the hens had laid. Every day we took water round.

The hen's eggs I used to put in big sacks and boil the hen's eggs up till they were hard in a copper. We had to shell all the eggs, then we had a big sieve turned upside down and we mashed the eggs through the sieve. All the food stuff (malted milk etc) was mixed up with the eggs and we used this to feed the young pheasants on.

And then as the pheasants got bigger we used to catch each one independently and put a strap on its wing so they couldn't fly away. They were all reared for food. Dwights, the butchers in Berkhamsted used to buy all the pheasants. Dwights came to break their necks and took them away. There were thousands of pheasants all over the hills October and November time.

George used to take a drink in a bottle to the Linces. One day when he wasn't there I thought I would sample it. I took a bit too much and knocked myself out and was asleep when he came back. He said "Don't you dare drink that, it's poison in there. I'll get a drink for you on its own," and he got me lemonade.

One day when we were sleeping in the hut George left his double barrel shotgun cocked. He reached out for his alarm clock and knocked the gun over. The gun went off and blew a hole through the corner of the hut.

MUM AND DAD'S WORK

Dad worked on Elsage Farm, the Sayell's farm, for years. When they sold out to H.A. Kempster & Son from Marsworth, Dad carried on working for him. After they got rid of the pheasants from Bishop's Farm I worked on Kempster's Farm (Elsage) until I left school at 14. Then I worked on Elsage farm full time. Our Mum cleaned houses for people and did washing. Cleaning St Giles' Church was hard work them days. No water was laid on she used to have to take it up. She boiled water in a kettle when electric was laid on.

WORKING AT CHEDDINGTON AIRFIELD

Sunleys first started the airfield off, then Wing airfield come about and Sunleys left Cheddington and went to Wing. W. Wimpey come in and developed Cheddington. Farmers with horse and carts worked on the airfield carting stuff around. I was officially working for Kempsters but he was contracted out to work for Wimpeys. Kempsters had no end of horses and carts down there. I had a horse and a four wheeled trolley on the airfield because I had several jobs to do. As they were concreting the runway they used to protect it with muslin cloth. After the concrete had dried out and was shining white (visible from the air) so one of the jobs I had was to drive the horse and trolley with the spraying machine on the back. It was hooked onto the trolley. Two Indians, who were deaf and dumb, worked the pump and the spray. I got on well with the Indians and I could explain what needed to be done. There were quite a few Indians working on the airfield, but many more Irish people.

Where the gypsies are now (Cheddington Lane, Long Marston), there were rows and rows of huts and the Irish working people were billeted there. There was a big canteen cooked all the meals there. Another of my jobs used to be in these huts and the canteen, there was old round stoves in there. I used to have to stock them up with coke and clean all the ashes away. No one told me where to put all the rubbish I collected, for example cardboard. I put it in a big heap in the corner near the Wash Brook, where Frazier's buildings are now. As the airfield started to get developed an RAF Wellington, with a damaged undercarriage from a bombing raid, crash landed and forced its way through my pile of rubbish and ended up on the Long Marston Road just the other side of Wash Brook. It was called Wash Brook because the farmers had a place on the side of the road for dipping sheep.

SEARCHLIGHT BATTERY

During the early part of the war there was a searchlight battery manned by the Army and anti-aircraft guns was in there. [It was situated on the Mentmore side of Long Marston Lane nearly one mile from Cheddington cross roads, Ed.] When the bombers come over, the searchlights played on them. There was quite a lot went on that people didn't know about.

Cheddington Control Tower

All that was left of Fortress '530' after it caught fire on take-off
from Cheddington. Aylesbury firemen attend the scene.

Royal Observer Corps Station

B-24 Liberator, background Westend Hill

MENTMORE PARK

Along Mentmore Park, on the grass verges, they cut the trees down and put the trunks on both sides of the grass verges and just left the road clear. The reason being was to prevent German gliders landing if there was an invasion. There was three bombs dropped in Mentmore Park. They dun't half shake us up. I always reckoned they were after Mentmore Towers. A gang of us went along there and were picking up the shrapnel. Sergeant King came along from Linslade Police Station and took the shrapnel away from us.

ARMY MANOEUVRES ON THE LINCES

Leading up to D-Day they had all these manoeuvres up on the north Linces. The tanks come through the fields from Mentmore and attacked the other lot [the opponents, Ed] on the Linces. You never seen such holes in the corn and hedges. The old farmers did go on about it. I don't know if they was compensated. It seemed a shame you was growing food for people and the tanks came through and ransacked it. I never see no tanks through Cheddington High Street. They were so wide they wouldn't have gone over the canal bridge. There was a lot of bren gun carriers they were on tracks. There were British troops all over Cheddington. In Manor Road we used to take them cups of tea out.

ROUGH LANDING FOR PROTOTYPE LANCASTER

As the airfield was being built the first runway (a short runway) was parallel to the Long Marston Road / Cheddington Lane. There was all the stuff for the runway (working stuff). At the Marston end there was a big concrete mixer on sleepers so you could drive underneath. What happened, the prototype of the Lancaster bomber got into difficulties and landed on this runway. He got right to the top where the concrete mixer was – he hit it and that soon stopped. This happened before we got to work this morning. (When we got to work at 7.30am) the Lanc was covered, the police and RAF were there. They kept us away from it. That was the first four engine plane people had seen. The crew from it – they stopped at The Rosebery Arms for several days. The RAF dismantled the plane and took it away on Queen Marys (transporters).

BLENHEIM BOMBER BLOCKS ROAD

During the early days of the war a Blenheim twin engine bomber crashed in South End field between the canal and the Linces. It was facing Cheddington and completely blocked the road. He didn't give himself enough room for landing, he come right through the hedge in between. The pilot was not badly hurt. What you had to do then to get out of the village, you had to go through the farmer's field and then come out the gate opposite Seabrook turn until the RAF dismantled the plane. The RAF rebuilt the plane in the field, it took several weeks. They were billeted in marquees in the field and slept in them to guard the plane. I watched the plane take off.

On West End Hill The Royal Observer Corps were based in a wooden hut. They had an RAF colour uniform to wear. They just had a phone for reporting German aircraft. They seemed to me to be the well-to-do people. There was Mr Barnes, a solicitor in London; Mr Heley from Ivinghoe; the Pennell brothers from Mentmore; the man from the Moat House [possibly now The Chase, Ed] and Mr Jeffery, the headmaster.

Just before the end of the war a big underground place was built on top of West End Hill, maybe put there as a shelter in case nuclear bombs were dropped.

CHEDDINGTON WATER WORKS – PUMPING STATION

In the early days of the war, the Water Works, which Wing District Council was in charge of, had to have sand bags put all round its outside walls so as to prevent damage in case of explosions near to it. The work for this was undertaken by Mr G. Alcock & Son of Cheddington, our local builder. He had a friend of mine working for him, Mr Ivor Bonham. He had just left school, he was to fill the bags up with sand and place them around the outside of the building. But while there working, Ivor thought he would watch the pump when it started up drawing water from the bore hole and pumping it into the water reservoir. But alas, just like all young people, he was tempted by the big pistons that went up and down by the cog wheels. Ivor put his hand onto the piston as it was working, then took his hand in between the piston rod and the cog wheel. It tore skin all off his hand. He was lucky he never had his hand off.

He was taken to Stoke Mandeville Hospital, this was when the Canadians and the sick and wounded from France were there. He had skin grafted from his stomach onto the back of his hand. He was a very lucky person and a grand mate of mine.

THE HOME GUARD

Mr Priest was in charge of the Home Guard and he lived opposite Town farm. His buildings was used for storage (ammunition, grenades). It was their headquarters. A lot got left there after the war and the bomb disposal squad was called to remove it.

The old hut we had on South End Hill, when the pheasants were all gone, was used by the Home Guard. It was placed where the old pond used to be and the Home Guard used to report there for duty at night. From there they used to go to the important spots – railway bridges and canals, so no one didn't go placing bombs.

Where the roundabout is now, at the crossroads, there used to be a grass piece, there was a gun emplacement surrounded by sandbags, metal tin covered the top. So you could see the four ways (to Mentmore, the station, Cheddington and Long Marston) you had to have holes to see and shoot through. The gun emplacement was used when they had exercises. It was there in case of attack. Six people could get inside.

The members of the Home Guard I remember are Bert Wesley who worked at Home Farm, Sid and Will Wesley, who worked for Mr Isaacs, Mr B. Brazier, Dick Wesley, Mr Dumpleton, my brother Fred Janes, Gilbert Norwood, Wilf Gilman, and Mr Tomilon. Bert and Sid Wesley were sergeants and Bill Wesley was a corporal, Bill used to have a paper round. In bad weather they used to do training and drill where the scout hut is now.

Derek Wesley and myself, we got in as messenger boys. We had to give messages from the headquarters (Mr Priest's place) by running to the different groups wherever they were on duty e.g. at bridges. There was no mobile phones in them days. It was a bit peculiar. It

was a good job Hitler never come, I don't think we would have lasted long!

THE ARP (AIR RAID PRECAUTIONS)

The headquarters of the ARP were at Mr Harold Perry's on The Green. He had a garage there for his car. They used to assemble there. They used to be on look out and check windows and doors to make sure you had no light shining through for the blackout.

THE FIRE SERVICE

The Fire Service was placed up the same yard (Masons). The Fire Service had one of the buildings where Masons keep the milk now as their headquarters. They were owned by Mr Williams.

Michael Chandler's dad Sammy and Reg Bishop (Eve Sharp's uncle) were in charge. All they was equipped with was stirrup pumps and buckets and buckets of sand. They didn't stand a chance if there was a fire. A rick of corn caught fire corner of Keepers Meadow and Southend Hill. It got set alight. The Cheddington Fire Service attended and could not manage it with only stirrup pumps so they had to call the Fire Service from a local town. All over the country ricks had to be built separately so not all the corn would be lost if incendiary bombs were dropped.

WVS (WOMEN'S VOLUNTARY SERVICE)

There was a WVS formed. I don't know who was on it. They used to preserve fruit and make pies to sell. They used to collect round for woollen gloves to send to the troops and things like that.

RAISING FUNDS FOR THE RETURNING TROOPS

During the war we used to run functions to raise money for a war memorial hall which was supposed to be built where part of the school is now, round the back where the school gardens were. We used to have classes for gardening them days. There was quite a sum of money raised from the events. But at the end of the war, when the boys were demobbed, they was asked whether they wanted the money cash in hand or the memorial and they said they would rather have the money. Long Marston done their memorial hall.

celebration of VE day was a good day. Everybody enjoyed theirselves. They had refreshments laid on.

THE END OF THE WAR

This was celebrated after VE Day in Cheddington because it all had to be organised. I was drinking a special brew come out, nice strong beer we used to call it Jungle Juice.

We had big celebrations in Cheddington. There were events for children, sack races and football organised on the recreation ground and village green. The village green was decorated up. There was four pubs in Cheddington and they was all open. (My mother's father, Mr Hill had The Old Swan in the early 1900s. My mum was only 16 when she come down from London to the Old Swan.) Michael Chandler's dad and Reg Bishop had an old barrel organ for going round pubs and playing. They was in charge of the organ on VE Day. They didn't do all the winding mind you, other people wound it. I helped down at the Swan. The

The old Keeper's/Shepherd's hut where Ivan used to sleep whilst guarding the pheasant on South End Hill. It was later moved and used by members of the Home Guard to report for duty.

The Home Guard Photo: We believe they are: Standing: ? / Eric Bonham?/ Dick Wesley? / Fred Pearce / William Wesley / Jack Newton / Dave Cook. Seated: Dick Frieth / Walter Heley / ? / William Rees, vicar? / Albert (or Sid) Wesley / Bill Brazier. If you know the others, or if we are wrong, please let us know!

Preparing for the Evacuees

From the Leighton Buzzard Observer, 24th January 1939:

CHEDDINGTON PARISH COUNCIL

The Evacuation Plans

A special meeting of Cheddington Parish Council was held on Friday to consider a letter from Wing Rural District Council on the evacuation of children from London.

Mr H Beilby, the local representative on the Rural Council, attended the meeting and explained that the Parish Council's duty was to appoint visitors to ascertain the amount of surplus accommodation on the basis of one person per habitable room.

The following enumerators were appointed, subject to their consent: Mrs F Jeffery, Mr G Alcock, Miss A Green, Mr T Blundell, Mrs R Tompkins and Mr A Fathers. The Chairman and the Clerk volunteered to see all of them. Mr Saxby, the rating officer, had asked for an up-to-date copy of the Village Register and the letter was sent to Col. G R Crouch.

Mr F S Jeffery gave notice of his intention to discuss the administration and distribution of the village charities at the next meeting.

An application was received for a Council House and the Chairman appealed to members to get in touch with people who were likely to require a house and forward the application to the Rural District Council.

Members present were Messrs G Alcock (Chairman), F Jeffery, F Chandler, A Wesley, W Boarder, A Beasley and the Clerk (Mr R H Tompkins).

From the Leighton Buzzard Observer in February 1939:

THE EVACUATION CANVASS

Accommodation More Limited Than Expected

The canvass of Leighton Buzzard and Linslade householders under the Government's evacuation scheme has now been completed, and there is reason to believe that the accommodation available for children to be sent out of London in the event of War is much smaller than was expected. The actual figures are, of course, a secret, but local inquiries show that in working class districts many householders have no spare accommodation, even on the high scale of one person per room laid down by the Home Office.

The attitude of most householders toward the scheme - and after all, they are the ones who will bear the brunt of any increase in household duties - is quite friendly; but the average working man occupies a cottage providing only the minimum accommodation for himself and his family. He cannot afford to pay rent for empty rooms. In families where there are several children there is more than one person per habitable room permanently living in the house.

Elderly people who are not able to undertake the care of young children are also more numerous than anyone suspected. People living in slightly larger houses have the greatest surplus accommodation, judged by the Home Office formula, but again a serious domestic problem has to be faced. The housewife who is proud of her home and keeps it spotlessly clean with the occasional help of a charwoman cannot be expected to look forward to taking in and catering for several children whose domestic habits may or may not be of her own standard. There is all round, however, a disposition to be helpful so long as good nature and patriotism are not imposed upon.

The average householder's view is well put by a Leighton Buzzard housewife, who said:- "There is too much of an emergency plan about the evacuation scheme. If this plan for bundling London children into neighbouring towns and villages - regardless of their military importance - is the best that the great brains of Whitehall have been able to devise, then we are not being too well served for all the money the nation is spending on public administration."

The Evacuees Arrive

From the Leighton Buzzard Observer September 5th 1939

LEIGHTON BUZZARD AND THE WAR
7,000 CHILDREN ARRIVE

Leighton Station Scenes

Leighton Buzzard Railway Station has seen the detraining during the past few days, of 7,000 children evacuated from London suburbs. The older children, who seemed to regard this experience as a holiday; younger children, who looked tired and bewildered; mothers and babies, and even expectant mothers, have come by successive trains. Their cheerfulness, even in face of long waits for billets, has been admirable, and has been contributed to in no small measure by the splendid work of local officials and voluntary workers. From the moment of stepping on to the railway platform, every evacuee has been made to feel cordially welcome.

Schoolchildren evacuated from London began to arrive in Leighton Buzzard on Friday morning, the first train, which came in at 11.45, bringing about eight hundred children.

For some time before the train pulled up at the platform the local evacuation officers were waiting in the Station approach, which was closed to the public. Thirteen buses were also waiting to move the children to the villages.

Leighton Station was one of the chief detraining centres in the county, and during the three days in which refugees arrived more than seven thousand people detrained.

The children were marshalled on the platforms by their teachers and marched into Linslade Recreation ground, passing thence through an office in Messrs. Tyler & Sons' timber yard for medical inspection before being allotted to the buses.

Scouts, Guides and other helpers saw that no child strayed from its party.

When the first train arrived it was so long that children in the front carriages had to be unloaded before the second part could be drawn up to the platform.

The children all came from the northern districts of London, and contrary to ill-founded rumours were very clean and tidy. Many of them, it was remarked, would probably go to homes which were not as good as their own. All the children carried their respirators and parcels or bags, and most of them seemed to regard the trip as the beginning of another holiday. Some of them brought sand pails and cricket bats. Each child wore a tied on ticket so that should any get lost they could be quickly identified.

The local St. John Ambulance Brigade and Nursing Division were in attendance, but there were no accidents.

A crowd of sightseers thronged the entrances to the Station and the Recreation Ground, but they were not allowed by the Special Constables and the regular police to get nearer. The police carried their gas masks and steel helmets.

The first bus to move off was to Marsworth which was loaded as soon as the children passed the doctor.

17

The work of sorting out the children was greatly helped by microphones and loud speakers, through which Mr. M.C.Clifford was able to call up the parties to the medical hut.

The first train carried 272 children for Leighton Buzzard, 38 for Marsworth, 34 for Pitstone, 96 for Wingrave, 80 for Totternhoe C.E. School, 35 for Totternhoe Memorial Hall and 250 for Dunstable.

THE SECOND PARTY

The second train was timed to reach Leighton about 2.30 p.m. but it did not arrive until 3.45, and brought much younger children, some of them under five years old. With their bundles they were a pathetic sight, and everyone rushed to carry them to the Recreation Ground. They stared wonderingly around all the time, and seemed to be rather bewildered.

Most of these children came from the Willesden district. Some 250 of them were counted off and sent straight to Dunstable. Only 54 for were kept for Leighton Buzzard. The remainder were sent to the villages. This party was dealt with much more speedily than the first. Fifteen buses carried the children to their temporary homes at Dagnall, Stanbridge, Hockliffe, Eggington, Soulbury, Cublington and Aston Abbotts.

All kinds of parcels were carried by these small evacuees. Some had kit bags which looked suspiciously like pillowslips. All appeared to be very tired. The huge task of evacuating London's millions of children has probably been underestimated.

On Friday morning Mr.W. S. Higgs, Chairman of Leighton Urban Council, commandeered all bedding and blankets from local shops, but there was still an urgent need for more and householders were asked to lend any spare blankets.

The task of allocating unaccompanied children has not proved very difficult, but there has been much trouble on housing mothers and children.

The ration handed to each child before being taken to billets was more than generous. Indeed, for tiny tots, a 1lb tin of beef, several tins of milk and a bag of biscuits seemed to be more than just a trifle absurd. But the authorities intentions were good and erred, if at all, on the right side.

HINTS TO HOUSEHOLDERS

Pamphlets on the care of evacuated children have been issued to householders by the Women's Voluntary Service.

The rate of payment is 10/6 for one child and 8/6 per child if more than one child is taken. The Billeting Officer will hand to the householder a form which can be cashed at the local Post Office. Payment will be made weekly in advance, and covers full board and lodging but not clothes or medical expenses.

Arrangements are being made to continue the children's education. This may mean that the schools will work in shifts. Schools in the district will not re-open until September 15th.

HOUSEHOLD DUTIES

BILLETED WOMEN MUST HELP
We are requested to point out that women billeted with their children are expected to assist with household duties and that any neglect or refusal to do so may have unpleasant consequences.

Evacuees arrive at Wing

Mr Jeffery, Headmaster of Cheddington School. Mr Jeffery played a big role in accommodating the varying numbers of evacuees at the school. (See the School Log Book extracts in Appendices.)

Stanley William Dunn

EVACUATED TO CHEDDINGTON

My father died in 1938. When he died we moved in with my Gran in Victoria Park, next to Hackney Wick and I went to Berkshire Road School. One day we got on a coach outside the school and we just came to Leighton Buzzard station, into a big pen place, maybe the cattle market. We were all nitted [hair and scalp was searched with a nit comb for evidence of nits, Ed]. Several coaches were there. I think it was a nice September day. It was pot luck where we were allocated and our coach went to Cheddington.

We walked into Cheddington School and we were organised from there. They had all these palliasses piled to the ceiling. Another thing I remember, we were each given a brown paper carrier bag containing provisions, e.g. a tin of corned beef etc.

LIFE AT ANDREWS TERRACE

We weren't true evacuees because we stayed with Mum. She was given 4 Andrews Terrace, a two up two down. We slept on the palliasses.

Mum then got some of her furniture down from London. In the end most of our London furniture came down, which was as well because later the house in London was bombed out and we lost what was there. In the meantime my Gran and Grandad had come to live with us and they lost everything left in the house. We went back to live in London during the phoney war when nothing happened for months and we returned to Cheddington when the bombing started, Gran and Grandad came too.

There was another house, number one, at the bottom of Andrews Terrace, my aunt acquired that and lived there with several of my cousins. At one stage there were eight to ten of us in our house, cousins, Mum, Gran and Grandad and us. In later years my uncle (William Hillyard) ran the Old Swan. During the war his son, Bill, stayed with us almost permanently. He returned to London but he thinks Cheddington is wonderful and sometimes regrets that he didn't stay here.

In the house in Andrews Terrace there was no electric and no running water. At the corner of The Green there was a standpipe and we used to get buckets of water. We had a flush toilet outside but no water in the house. The oil lamps blackened the ceilings and it was a constant battle trying to keep the ceiling a bit decent. I think we had water and electricity by the end of the war.

VILLAGE SHOPS

The village then had two main shops Mrs Turner (where George Mason's son lives now) and Tappy May's. Also the Masons (George and Horace's father) lived where the garage is now, they had sheds at the back and they sold paraffin and globes for the lamps. Every now and then they used to get a box of bananas. Also at the front they had a petrol pump – but there weren't many cars about. Halfway down Blenheim Hill, on the left [the same side as The Three Horseshoes] was a coal yard. There was a coalman there. He used to also charge radio batteries, they were called accumulators. You took the old one in and would exchange it for a charged one. We used to have a baker, Irving Gower, by The Green, opposite the bus shelter.

UNWILLINGLY TO CHAPEL!

Of course we used to go to the Methodist Chapel at that time on the village green (not willingly). The chapel was run by Miss Beilby.

GOING TO THE VILLAGE SCHOOL

We went to the village school, the village hall (now the scout hut) was used for overflow pupils. Mr Jeffery was the headmaster during the war. On Irving's Linces they had an observers post. Mr Jeffery was one of the observers. Some nights he had to spend the night up there and didn't have enough sleep. He could be grumpy at school after a night watching for enemy aircraft. Mr Jeffery had a lot to put up with but by and large he ran a good ship. He did cane (cut from a bush out the back of the school), but I wouldn't say he was particularly hard.

On occasion Mr Jeffery's wife came in and helped out a bit. They were desperate for teachers during the war – everyone was. The infant teacher was Miss Alderman – she was very nice too. We used to have a garden at the school at the back. We used to do a bit of gardening. One of my cousins referred to a spade as a shovel and the country boys thought calling a spade a shovel was hilarious.

THE HOME GUARD

Right opposite Miss Beilby's house was a bit of grassland with a big hut on wheels. The LDV (Local Defence Volunteers) hut – the Home Guard operated from there. We had a character in the village called Lal Wesley. He was very good with his hands and he used to build aircraft out of cocoa tins. One Spitfire had a wingspan of six feet and was camouflaged, you would think it was professionally made. He was in the Home Guard. He was the fit one amongst all the old men. During the war the Army did manoeuvres and we had tanks in the village and Army personnel.

WATCHING THE AMERICANS FROM THE LINCES

After school (we had no TV and the radio wasn't that great) we roamed the fields. Once the Americans were here we used to sit in the Linces and watch the gliders going up. The Dakotas took off, circled and released the gliders. I would imagine that we would have been under observation. We used to spend a lot of time up there.

CATCHING RABBITS IN MENTMORE SPINNEY

When we first came down here the locals used to have a bit of a go at us. When we said we couldn't catch rabbits they told us to put salt on the rabbit's tail. So we used to chase the rabbits with a packet of salt in Mentmore spinney, much to the amusement of the local lads! We all had short trousers on and the

stinging nettles were up to your waist and we got stung to high heaven. The penny dropped eventually.

LEARNING TO PLAY BASEBALL

Another thing that changed in the village was when the Americans came, there was one occasion when we were playing cricket and two Americans came along on their bikes "What's this game you're playing?" they asked. When we told them it was cricket they said "You don't wanna play cricket you wanna play baseball." The next afternoon they came over with a baseball bat and equipment and taught us to play their game. I still remember parts of what they told us, I know you have to hit the ball forward and not behind you. The Americans were very friendly. We used to ask them "Have you got any gum chum?" and they gave us the American gum which was in strips and more superior to our spearmint gum.

ANDREWS TERRACE AT END THE OF WAR

By the end of the war Mum had married an Irish man, Francis Power, who worked on the aerodrome building it. He lived with us at number 4 too. So in Andrews Terrace we had cousins in numbers 1 and 7. The Gilmans lived at number 5. After them in about 1945/46 the Kehoes moved in. Ted Kehoe used to cut our hair.

SETTLING IN CHEDDINGTON AFTER THE WAR

When the war ended Mum was keen to go back to London. We actually went back in 1945. We lived with my Gran for about a year. It was a time when Sheila's Cottage won the Grand National. It was the year we weren't very well, there were smogs in London. You couldn't get a house, so many people had been bombed out. It was all renting, so we returned to Cheddington.

Looking back now I am eternally grateful we came back to Cheddington because I think we had a better life in the country. Fate is a funny thing. I wouldn't have met my wife if we had not come back.

Audrey Purr

HAVING EVACUEES WAS CHAOS!

In 1939, at the beginning of the war – 'The phoney War' before the bombing started – we had two sisters; Doris, 14 and Betty, seven. Betty cried all the time she was with us – two or three months. Doris cried for days because she had to go home!

William Ellis School, Camden, was evacuated to Leighton Buzzard.

We had four boy evacuees :

1. Laurence Hogstead, aged fifteen, who was a different lad to the others. He would stand in the kitchen cleaning his riding boots and if he went to the shop he would take an umbrella. He stayed to take his exams.

2. Gordon Cornwall had black, curly hair.

3. Roy Shaw lived there for eighteen months and finished his exams. I am still in touch with him. He became Leader of Camden Council and was Mayor of Camden Town in 2000.

4. Harry was very disruptive at school but behaved at home. His brother, Matt Munro, came to visit me.

Afterwards we had RAF people. Paddy Ward after that. It was like having older brothers and sisters and they were good to me. I used to get in the van of the WAAF with the driver.

Extract from the Leighton Buzzard Observer, 28th January, 1941

EVACUEES' BOOTS AND CLOTHING
WING RURAL COUNCILLORS COMPLAINTS
FOSTER PARENTS' DIFFICULT POSITION
HAVE TEACHERS FAILED?

Complaints of unreasonable delay in providing clothing and boots for evacuated children whose parents cannot be traced, were made by members of Wing Rural District Council on Tuesday. It was stated that teachers had been told by the County Education Committee to watch such cases and to bring them to the notice of the London County Council's care committee, and that evacuated teachers should have noticed these cases.

One member said that foster parents who could not afford the expense had bought boots for the children because they could not bear to see them going about in worn-out boots in such weather. Mr J.M. Lyon raised the question by asking what was to happen to children whose parents could not be traced. The Clerk (Mr. M.C. Clifford) replied that the first duty of the teacher, if the parents could not be found, was to get into touch with the London County Council welfare department which would meet the accounts. The teacher must make the first approach to the L.C.C.

Joyce Ginzel
(HORTON)

OUR EVACUEES
We had a lot of evacuees come and stay from London and I am still in touch with Don. Near the end of the war his mother and father came with his baby sister Margaret. She was being fed on tinned milk but not gaining weight but we put her on our cow's milk and she soon picked up. His father would only be here for the weekend as he was a trolley bus driver in the week.

The three Irish nurses who stayed with Joyce Ginzel at Horton

NURSES, A SPY AND SQUADRON LEADER'S WIFE!
I remember having 3 Irish nurses, another lady whose husband was a squadron leader. We also had a spy. They had a bedroom and back sitting room. He was supposed to be doing something with the aerodrome. His wife had an accent which I think was Russian. They had a little girl but she was never allowed out. We didn't think anything of it although I think my mother suspected something was not right. He kept a trunk in our cow sheds.

We had the police come and pick up all their stuff and they were picked up in London. There was also strange goings on at the time at Hortondene, the occupants were picked up by the police never to be seen again. Other evacuees used to arrive, some stayed a short time, others longer. I am not sure how they got in touch with us.

AIR RAID IN LONDON
I went up to London once with Don's mum and we had an air raid while I was there. We had to go out to the shelter. The noise of the guns was horrendous. Everything shook. I don't know how they put up with it night after night.

AMMUNITION FROM COLONEL SHAND KYDD
Colonel Shand Kydd went to London and brought back 11 rifles, 1 machine gun, 2 pistols and grenades and all the ammunition to fit the guns and we stored it all at our house. We kept 2 pistols and a box of grenades at the top of our stairs. I am surprised we didn't go up. I learnt to shoot a German pistol when I was eight. I never played with dolls I use to clean the guns. I knew all the parts of the Thompson gun and how it all went together. After the war we still had sacks of ammunition and guns under our stairs and they came and took it all back.

CUNNING PLAN TO WATCH BOMB DISARMED
We're supposed to have had three bombs dropped near here. Only two were ever found. Jack Shorter of Old Farm Horton had just built his corn and hay ricks and a bomb exploded in the middle of them. Another landed by an oak tree outside here but never went off. It made a big hole and they put barbed wire around it. When they came to disarm it we were all told to stay in. A boy who lived in the cottage next door and I devised a cunning plan. We both said we were around each other's houses but we met and crept through to watch. Nobody saw us and if it had gone off nobody would have known where we were.

From left to right: Joyce's grandfather, Joyce, Don, an Irish nurse, Joyce's mother, Mrs Grant (Don's mother) setting off on a shopping trip to Leighton Buzzard

MANOEUVRES IN HORTON

We had manoeuvres going on in Horton. Not sure where they came from. They had built a Bailey bridge over the canal. We had a big chicken house near the road and they parked a tank behind it. They used to camp at the old barn in Horton and we used to sell them eggs. I have no idea what they were doing. When they went we found loads of tins of biscuits.

SING SONG WITH UNCLE'S PALS

My uncle was based in Wing and he was a photographer who used to photo the sights where they would drop the agents. He used to bring his pals here and I would sometimes play the piano to them.

Sometimes the Americans would come and we would have a good old sing song. Some of my uncle's pals we would see again and others we never did see again. My uncle use to say "If I'm not back by nine, don't expect me!"

GERMAN AIR CREW PUT FEAR OF GOD IN ME!

I hated school and one day I was biking there and I saw three German aircrew coming along the road. I went past them and never peddled so fast in my life. They really put the fear of God in me.

BUT CUPS OF TEA FOR THE RAF!

Early in the war we had 2 airplanes land in the field at the back. They were RAF flyers. They walked down to our house and had a cup of tea. and then they took off again.

NEVER A DULL MOMENT BUT NO PROBLEMS

There never seemed a dull moment, there was always something going on. We always felt safe here. There were always troops about but we never bothered to lock our doors. We sometimes went to Leighton and did our shopping in the pony and trap. My cousin from Slapton and I use to walk miles by ourselves. We use to see Americans going by on bikes and see Army trucks. We use to go to Long Marston and watch the aeroplanes take off and walk to Leighton and would not get back until it was dark but we never worried. No one seemed to cause any problem here.

Miriam Mason

THE THREE HORSESHOES

My grandmother had died young and when her father remarried, my mother Evelyn Tomsin, 'Tom', who had not got on well with her new step-mother, went to live with her grandparents, Annie and Reginald ('Bap') Cook at The Three Horseshoes.

They brought her up and she lived there until she married my father, Fred Atkins, from Leighton Buzzard. He was a groom for Mr Stoddart and after they were married they went to live at number 3, which was a tied cottage next to the Police House.

I was born in 1938 at 3 Church Lane, but when I was about two years old we moved to The Three Horseshoes to live with my great grandmother after Bap died. My great grandmother was called 'Auntie' by everyone.

In those days our living quarters were downstairs. Our living room was where the toilets are now. The Tap Room was uncarpeted with red tiles, and it was where the locals went. Now it's the Saloon Bar. The lavatories were outside and the bedrooms were upstairs. There was a large bedroom upstairs, with a fireplace, and this was made into a bed-sit for my great grandmother. My mother always used to cook the meals and my great grandmother had her meals with us but there was always the private time when she wanted it.

MOTHER PLAYED THE PIANO

My mother played the piano in the Bar every night and the Yanks used to come up from the aerodrome and join in the singing. Later the R.A.F. came - at the end of the war.

I knew some of the Americans. One of them, Roger, who was married, used to stay with us when he had his 48-hour leave. He told his wife about us and she used to send a big parcel at Christmas with presents. I remember a red knitted hat with a tassel and red mittens to match – and candies, and nylons for my mother. I also remember that once there was a bag of flour in the parcel and it had broken and there was flour over everything.

The piano was in what is now the Public Bar and it used to be packed. It was noisy and smoky. The window used to be open – at least, in the summer.

There was one called Freece who was a cook at the camp and for some of the village girls who used to come up, he used to make a birthday cake for them. It was really gooey and the icing was different to ours.

HIDING THE BREN GUN

There was another one (American) called Ben Cotton – a very tall person. One day there was three or four of them came up the road in a bren gun carrier. There was a black thatched barn up near the house. One came in and said to my mum,

"Do you think you can hide this?"

They managed to get it between the barn and the house round by the back door so that if any MPs (Military Police) came by they wouldn't see it as they weren't meant to be there.

ROADBLOCK

The ground opposite the Horseshoes was part of the Horseshoes and my father had a vegetable garden there, with a five-bar gate. When the Yanks were doing an exercise they used to make a roadblock by taking our gate off its hinges and, with rolls of barbed wire, block the road.

LATE FOR SCHOOL

The pub closed at 10 o'clock but my parents had to tidy up and hand-wash all the glasses so they were quite late to bed and I was always late for school.

My teacher was Winnie Alderman. There was only two classes. She lodged with the Headmaster and his wife, Mr and Mrs Jeffery, at the schoolhouse. She was nice.

MOTHER PLAYED PIANO IN WILLESDEN STREET!

We had relations in London, in Willesden, and because my mother could play the piano, they asked her to go up and play the piano in the street and I went with her – probably on VE Day as I can't remember VE Day in Cheddington. They had a grocery shop. There was long tables for the children. I remember sitting with my second cousins and having sandwiches, jelly and cakes and things. They sang 'Little Brown Jug', 'Daisy Daisy', 'Knees Up Mother Brown', 'Pack Up Your Troubles' and 'Tipperary'.

Amanda Miscampbell

BATTLE OF THE RIVER PLATE

Seeing a picture of the River Plate game made me think of my grandfather who was an Operations Intelligence Officer on the cruiser 'Ajax' in the Battle of the River Plate in December, 1939. Churchill said it was a great victory that "in a cold and dark winter warmed the cockles of our hearts."

GRANDAD MENTIONED IN DESPATCHES

My grandad was Mentioned In Despatches as a result he stayed on the South American station for two more years. He commanded the 'Beagle' in 1942 and was in the Arctic. In 1943 he was loaned to the Royal Canadian Navy and in 1944 he was Staff Officer (Operations) in the Med.

GRANNY AWARDED MBE

My Granny, who was a great character, was a First Officer WRNS and got an MBE in 1944 for her work as a Senior Cypher Officer, Plymouth Command, during Operation Neptune.

John T Smith

HOVE

I lived in Hove, Sussex, and was two when the war began. My father had served in the RAMC in the First World War, in the second he did firewatching duties at the fire station.

'FLAMING ONIONS!'

I have two distinct war memories - seeing 'flaming onions' across the sky, and hiding one morning with my mother and sister in the steel Morrison shelter in one of the downstairs rooms during an air raid. A bomb landed in the next street to us and demolished a house.

STRAFED BY A FIGHTER AEROPLANE

A school friend lived with his family above their butcher's shop, and access from the outside was up a long steel staircase over the back garden. During one raid his mother was going up the steps when the gardens were strafed by a fighter aeroplane, but she was left unscathed.

VICTORY PARADE

I watched the victory parade from the flat above a shop in one of the main streets of the town, Church Road.

MORRISON SHELTERS

Having looked up the Morrison shelter, I find that it was about 6 ft 6 ins by 4 ft and 2 ft 6 ins high, had a solid 1/8th steel plate top, with steel mesh sides and floor, and it came with three tools to assemble it from 359 individual parts! And it seems that 'flaming onions' were either flares or tracer ammunition or anti-aircraft fire.

Elsie Bonham

RON RICKARD'S SISTER

'SON'

My husband's uncle, Horace Tompkins, was killed in 1918 during the war. My husband was named after this uncle. When he was only two hours old my husband's grandfather picked him up and said "Come along son, let's have a look at you." From this point, my husband was known as 'Son'.

MY WORK

When the Second World War began I worked in the mantle factory owned by Corby, Palmer and Stewart in Berkhamsted. We made cardigans and costumes. Later I worked at Apsley Mills, Hemel Hempstead because they wanted war workers. The train drivers used to stop at Cheddington Station and wait for late people who were catching the train. One day, at Apsley Mills, I watched a dog fight; Spitfires were chasing bombers. I thought that I was too near London and that's when I decided to work at Gossards in Leighton Buzzard. Gossards made parachutes for airmen. I was employed on the four-needle machine, sewing the hems of parachutes. When we ran out of work hemming I helped with making the packs for the parachutes. This was mainly hand sewing.

MARRIAGE TO 'SON'

I was married to Son (Horace) on January 6th 1940, at Mentmore. His uncle Reg was an undertaker and his mother was Edith Tompkins. Their father lived in Cheddington Cottages, which were located where Chaseside Close is now. There were three cottages there. Miss Parodi lived in the end one nearest the Three Horseshoes, Fred and Emma Harrison lived in the middle and William and Emily Bonham lived in the third one. We lived with Son's Mum and Dad in New Street.

'SON' CALLED UP

On 15th January 1940 Son was called up. He was twenty-one. We thought we would get a few months

of married life together but we had been married less than a week when he had his calling up papers. It wasn't too bad until he got sent abroad. In the interim period after being called up and going overseas, for four or five months he was stationed in the army in Leighton Buzzard helping to start a Clearing Station. The station was located at Stockgrove House, then owned by Colonel Kielberg, between Heath and Leighton Buzzard. Son had laboratory experience at Tunnel Cement, Pitstone, so he got put in the Royal Army Medical Corps. He ended up in India. From Mandalay in Southern India he walked to Burma.

Horace 'Son' Bonham

SON'S SERVICE IN ROYAL ARMY MEDICAL CORPS

He was a nurse, often assisting and actually operating on the sick and injured. On one occasion Son operated on a Gurkha who believed Son had saved his life. He offered Son either his kukri (knife/sword) or a tiger's tooth necklace – both considered by Gurkhas as their most prized possession. Son chose the kukri. On at least three occasions the Japanese surrounded their camp. Every soldier in the camp was instructed to tie their shoe laces a certain way and any soldier who had not done this, i.e. a Japanese soldier, would be instantly decapitated by the Gurkhas and their head placed on a pole in the camp.

On one occasion, Son was holding down a soldier while the surgeon was amputating his leg with little or no anaesthetic. The soldier pushed Son away so fiercely that he was thrown to the other side of the tent where he hit a live electric wire on his forehead. The degree of electricity he received should have killed him.

For the rest of his life he had a red mark on his forehead.

MAKING PARACHUTES AT GOSSARDS
During the time I worked at Gossards in Leighton Buzzard making parachutes, the girls said,

"Where is it you live in Cheddington?"

I told them we lived at numbers 4 and 5 New Street. They then produced a piece about Son which had been printed in the local paper.

Leighton Buzzard Observer

BLOOD TRANSFUSION

LEIGHTON BUZZARD STATION'S WORK IN BURMA

When the 36th Division entered the Aeyarwaddy (my spelling) River port of Katha, in Burma, they found the once colourful town almost empty, neglected and dirty and overgrown with weeds and semi-jungle. The Japanese had done nothing to keep the town clean.

A casualty clearing station, which was formed in Leighton Buzzard in 1940, took over one of the largest bungalows and quickly transformed the locality.

This clearing station, which has operated in Arakan, Kohima, and is now with the 36th Division, lost only 39 men among the thousands of cases handled. Cpl Douglas Hall, of Oakley Green, Windsor, a former greyhound trainer, is in charge of the medical ward, and the blood transfusion expert is Cpl. Horace Bonham, of 5, New Street, Cheddington, who helped to give 400 blood transfusions during the two months of the Kohima battle. He is a laboratory assistant in peace-time.

The chief clerk, who deals with the records of the thousands of cases which have passed through the station, is Sergt. Ronald Simpson, of 48, Kings Road, Hitchin.

These men, and others, have handled up to 100 cases in one day. At Kohima none of them had more than one meal a day and each man worked in 12 hour shifts

----

It told about the work he was doing in India. He was assisting a surgeon called Thomas Fitt (nick-named Tom Tit), dealing with the Front Line sick until the war finished. Son enjoyed working with the injured. He would have hated being in a fighting regiment. He hated the thought of killing people, but he did have to carry a gun in Burma for his own safety, even though he was a non-combatant. He was a quiet man.

We used to have a band of women in the village who knitted garments like gloves and socks for the troops.

Son was demobbed on his 27th birthday, 19th March, 1946, at Northampton, but he came back to England shortly before then. I used to go to the Burma Star Association Dinners twice a year.

In July 1951 Son was called up for two weeks refresher training at Salisbury Plain, near Tilshead.

When Son was demobbed we lived in a cottage next to the Methodist Church, on The Green.

Marlene Lee

HEMEL HEMPSTEAD

WAR DECLARED

I can remember well the Sunday when war was declared. It was my father's 28th birthday and I was five years old. The next thing I recall is sleeping for weeks on a bed made under the stairs, learning to tell the different sounds of 'ours' and 'theirs' as the planes droned overhead and Londoners suffered the nightly blitz. I remember standing in the garden and seeing the glow in the sky the night when London was nearly burnt to the ground.

'DOING OUR BIT' AT SCHOOL

I lived in Hemel Hempstead and went to George Street School where the headmistress soon had us involved and 'doing our bit' to help the war effort. We were encouraged to save our pennies to buy six penny savings stamps at school every Monday morning. These were then exchanged for fifteen shilling Savings Certificates. We felt quite rich when we had accumulated a few of these.

The headmistress also organised a competition to see which pupil could collect the most jam jars, these would then be re-used at the jam factory. I was lucky enough to call on an elderly lady who found a bathful of cobwebby jars in her cellar, so I won the competition. The prize was a stick of rather soft, pre-war barley sugar (never my favourite sweet) but I felt quite important receiving it.

NO MORE IRON MOULD ON MY KNICKERS!

Randall's Park was one of our playgrounds but at the start of the war all the lovely iron gates and railings were removed and taken away to be melted down plus an ancient cannon that we played on. I think my mother was quite pleased about that because she was always saying "You have been on that old cannon again, there is iron mould all over your knickers."

The grass in the park was allowed to grow for hay and when this was cut we had a grand few days playing with it until it was carted away to a local farm.

After the hay it was soon harvest time and with my mother I would go gleaning. This is picking up the ears of corn left in the field after the reapers have finished. It was a hot, slow, prickly job but the corn was welcomed by our neighbour who kept hens and with whom we were registered for eggs.

After gleaning came rosehip picking – another prickly task. These were delivered to the hospital where I believe they were made into rosehip syrup for the vitamin C content. Next it was time for acorn gathering, when we collected baskets full for the local pigs. Another task was picking blackberries which were cooked up with apples and made into jam. When winter came we all went wooding as this helped out the meagre coal ration, there being only the one fire to warm the house.

TREATS FROM MY FATHER

In 1942 my father, now in the RAF, was sent via Durban, Cape Town and Malta to Italy. Soon parcels of almonds, walnuts and dried figs began to arrive. My mother didn't quite know what to do with the figs, but of all things to combine them with she chose rhubarb and made fig and rhubarb jam. It was a rather yucky looking dark brown, stringy mixture but I absolutely loved it.

Dad also sent us boiled sweets from his ration but couldn't send chocolate, so this he used to give to the orphanage. (He said later the children had so little.) In return the nuns gave him little cards and religious tracts with pictures of the local saint. These he sent home and I still have.

MORE BUZZ BOMBS AND THEN THE END OF THE WAR

The years moved on, the buzz bombs came over and again we would dash under the stairs and pray the engine wouldn't stop until it was over open country.

My father was injured but came home safely but not until after VE Day and VJ Day bonfires and parties had come and gone. The War finished on 15th August, 1945 and in September I began a whole new life as I moved from George Street School to the Hemel Hempstead Grammar School.

Albert Grimshaw

1939 when war broke out Stockport, Cheshire. Twenty four, joined Grenadier Guards stationed at Windsor. Used to watch Queen Mother, the present Queen and Princess Margaret - used to ride round on bicycles inside castle grounds. Queen Mother always said, "Good Morning Sentry."

Then went to Wellington Barracks, London.

Then to Wanstead Flats.

Then went to Wiltshire, training on Churchill Tanks.

Sailed over to France D-Day + 10.

Went from France to Belgium and Holland. Crossed the Rhine into Germany – war was getting to a close. Stationed Lubeck on the Baltic. War was over then.

Got back home, from being stationed in Munster, Eifel. Demobilised in 1946. Got back home by boat and landed at Portsmouth.

Awarded the Military Cross for bravery in the field.

[L/Sgt Albert Grimshaw was awarded his medal for the destruction of two German self propelled guns, Ed.]

Allan Glendinning

LIVERPOOL

SIRENS IN CITY CENTRE

We lived about six miles from the city centre and in September 1940 my mother, who must have been four months pregnant at the time with my twin brothers, and I travelled into the city. I recall it was dark and suddenly the air raid siren sounded. We sought safety in the nearest shelter which was in the vaults of St George's Hall. The area was full of people and I remember a stranger giving me a currant bun. The 'all clear' sounded and we left our shelter to seek transport to travel home. The sirens went again and by this time we were close to Exchange Station where we were able to find another shelter where we remained for the night. My only memory of this is the sandbags at the entrance. Eventually, the 'all clear' sounded again and we went for the No 43 tram to take us home. I cannot recall seeing any obvious signs of bomb damage. However just after the tram passed Anfield – the home of the city's most famous football team – in the distance across Stanley Park we could see an orange glow in the sky as the enemy target had been the docks which were now ablaze. We arrived home to find my father, a policeman, who had also been out all night, at the gate anxiously looking out for us. I also remember on another occasion travelling past St George's Hall during the day and seeing on the plateau outside the Hall two German aeroplanes which had been shot down and were presumably on show as a morale booster for the public.

UNDER THE TABLE WITH MY GRANDMOTHER

My next vivid memory is when my mother was in hospital giving birth to my twin brothers. I was at home under the care of my grandparents. I was actually under the table with my grandmother whilst my grandfather sat in an armchair. The sirens had sounded and I could hear the noises of the battle in the night. Suddenly there was an extra loud explosion and our lights went out. The 'all clear' duly sounded and after breakfast I walked the fifteen minutes to school. Incidentally on the way to school it was quite normal to walk past an anti-aircraft gun surrounded by sandbags and emergency water supply (EWS) tank. I soon ascertained the reason for the extra loud explosion. A bomb had dropped only half a mile from our home but fortunately had landed outside a church narrowly avoiding a number of houses. We had great fun running to the bottom of the crater and out again. The bomb had actually passed through the electricity wires thus putting the district into darkness. I'm not aware of any loss of life from this incident - just a number of broken windows.

ONE OF OUR SHELLS ATTACKS OUR HOME

This time we were in the Anderson air raid shelter in the back garden and again the noises of battle filled the air. There was a sudden whistling sound followed by an explosion very close to home. This was followed by a faint sound of running liquid and my mother shouted "It's an oil bomb - we are trapped." A neighbour at the back called out "Are you all right?" My father shouted that we were, although my mother was in a state of panic. In fact, what had happened was that a shell from one of our guns had landed in our front garden and had gone through the drain cover. What my mother had heard was running water. Some of the shrapnel actually penetrated the front door and hit my father's police helmet which was hanging up in the hall. Incidentally, from the Anderson shelter on one occasion I can recall seeing a German plane, very high in the sky, being attacked by our artillery.

EXTRAS FROM THE DOCKS

My policeman father's duties were essentially on the docks and we were fortunate that in the time of rationing we had the benefit of a few extras after he had made friends with the chief stewards on some of the visiting ships. One day he arrived home with a pure white loaf which looked magnificent compared with the usual grey bread to which we had become accustomed. Surprisingly I have to say that I felt no sense of fear during the various incidents, no doubt that was because of my tender years.

A bomb crater in Scotland Road, Liverpool,
May 1941

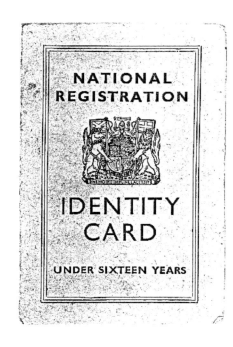

An Identity card issued to all British
citizens. This is the 'under sixteen' version
which would have been given to Allan.

Neil Castle

ARRIVAL AT THE OLD SWAN JANUARY 1939

My father, Bert, a Master Draper with a shop in Aylesbury, found he could not compete when Woolworths arrived, so he took over the tenancy of The Old Swan in January 1939. With my mother and five children, aged from 2 yrs to 14 yrs he soon had to prepare for another world war. He was only 47 years of age.

The preparations included digging an air-raid shelter in the front drive – within two days it was full of water – and constructing a black-out porch over the pub entrance. There was an air raid siren at Pitstone cement works. I heard its wail only once.

Our home was very special, with an inglenook fireplace, five bedrooms, two staircases and spooky cupboards under the eaves of the thatched roof. All the bedrooms had sloping walls and the scurrying of rats and mice could be heard through the lath and plaster walls. My younger sister, Phyllis, was given a guinea pig and one morning she found a rat had moved in with it! A man brought four kittens which we kept, and I named my tortoiseshell Joseph – with its coat of many colours – it soon produced a litter, so was renamed Josephine. But, despite all those cats we still had mice!

RUNNING WILD IN CHEDDINGTON

I was 7 yrs old, the third son, and soon found that lax parental supervision allowed me to run wild in the fields and orchards. With Jim Perry, Bob Whitehead, Mike Chandler, Norman Pollard, Leslie Dumpleton and other boys of my age we roamed far and wide, with bows and arrows, becoming the antagonists of the local farmers and especially of Mr Groves, the gamekeeper. We had arrived at a unique village which included a canal, a high-speed, steam, railway station and unfortunately, a small school.

WAR DECLARED

I believe I can remember the BBC announcement of the declaration of war, and we children were aware that Cheddington men were enlisting. I experienced a feeling of security when I heard uniformed men singing in the bar; and young as I was, the confidence that the British Empire would win.

Dad received posters from the Ministry of Information, about Air Raid Precautions, but I didn't take much notice of adults until a Local Defence Volunteer group was formed – later to be dubbed 'Dads' Army'. One day, the volunteers were given a demonstration of 'Incendiary Bombs, and How to Extinguish Them' in the meadow behind The Swan. I cautiously watched from a distance as military men attempted to ignite an ex-London bomb with a plumber's blow-lamp. Of course, the high temperature wasn't achieved and the show never started.

BOMB DAMAGE

But on one memorable night two landmines were jettisoned from an enemy plane onto Mentmore crossroads and it was a wonder that The Old Swan did not crumble from the vibration. Long Marston school had a direct hit, by a bomb, and a young teacher was killed. Mr. Gregory, the butcher, in his nearby shop, claimed he did not hear it but suddenly noticed that he could see daylight between his ceiling and the wall – the roof had lifted. At another time, a string of bombs fell on Mentmore spinneys, killing a sheep. So the war had arrived on Cheddington's doorstep.

GUESTS AT THE OLD SWAN

My mother, Ada, soon began to let two bedrooms for B&B and these paying guests added to the characterful locals who came to the bar. There were three pubs in the village and The Rosebery Arms Hotel, but The Old Swan was used by the tenant farmers and although trade was steady the rationing of supplies meant that Dad developed his own system of priority catering for the 'regulars'.

There were customers who could drink a pint of 'mild & bitter' in the time it took to select their change from the cash drawer. The clientele was almost totally male but changes crept in as women's position in society gradually rose. I was very smitten by five London nurses, who frequently came down from London to get away from 'The Blitz'. Somehow, the word that the girls had arrived travelled around the village and young men arrived to sing-along and dance with them.

The Air Ministry requisitioned land, in 1941, to construct an airfield behind the lynchets and a gang of navvies began to remove a power pylon, and bury some of the electric power cables which ran through the village. They drank a lot of beer in our pub but did not bother to remove their muddy boots. Whilst construction was proceeding we had a guest, Mr. WFC Brown, stay with us. He had a Ford car and was a surveyor of the sub-contract building work. He told Dad that he had been a member of the British Fascist Party, and was interned for a few weeks, sleeping on straw on a cell floor.

We also accommodated Albert Welsh who had been directed by The War Ministry to move south, from Market Harborough, to run the Tring Cutting signal box of the LMS railway system. Both men became almost adopted by our family, and Mrs. Welsh came down for weekend visits.

FOOD RATIONING

Food rationing worsened and a pig-swill bin was located near the water stand-pipe, outside Tompkins' store shed. Dad cultivated the gardens and Mum acquired chickens, ducks and geese, but soon it was difficult to obtain sugar, fats and other commodities. Irving Gower was the village baker with premises near The Old Inn, on The Green. He was, however, a regular customer at The Swan. Stories circulated of inedible items being found in the loaves and Irving being found asleep in the wooden flour mixing bin.

Dad volunteered to store paper salvage in the loft above the Swan garage, for the war effort. It was due to be collected but never was, I wonder whether it is still there!

THE VILLAGE SCHOOL

My elder brothers, Alan and Raymond, took Phyllis and me to enroll at the School. Alan was over six feet tall and wore a suit, making a good impression on Mr. Frank Sidney Jeffery, the Headmaster. There were three classrooms, Mrs Jeffery ran the middle room and an elder schoolgirl, named Barbara Dyer, took the youngest group, including me. There were two playgrounds; and a number of quaint children's games thrived in the small one, at the rear. The games were very active and even educational, in that quick decisions and reactions were essential, to avoid being strangled by skipping ropes, or injured during 'British Bulldog' – I still have the scars. During several summers, groups of schoolchildren were escorted to dig up dandelion roots, and pick wild rosehips from the meadows and hedges, again, 'for the war effort'.

AIRCRAFT RECOGNITION LESSONS FROM MR JEFFERY

Mr Jeffery was a member of the local Royal Observer Corps and would often insert an 'Aircraft Recognition' class for the boys and we became expert at identifying planes not only by their shape but also by their engine note. A Handley Page Harrow crash landed on Kingham's farm, the far side of the railway tracks. The next morning I went with several others to crawl over the outside and inside. Eventually, we remembered we should be at school. On arriving I was horrified to see those who had returned earlier lined up in Mr. Jeffery's classroom. He walked up and down the line with a cane in his hand, and we were resigned to being thrashed - corporal punishment was rife. He waited for the last stragglers to arrive, then said "Well, what type of aircraft was it?" And that was all. He was probably chuffed that we knew our stuff!

Earlier, I had witnessed the first plane crash, when a yellow Tiger Moth circled around, at fairly low level. Its engine was spluttering and it disappeared toward St. Giles church. My elder brother, Alan, and Alf Wesley, ran around Home Farm, behind the school and into the orchard near Church Walk and could see the flames above the wreckage. They pulled the Fleet Air Arm pilot from the cockpit and propped him against a plum tree. When he asked "How's Mickey?" they searched for another airman – until they saw a picture of Mickey Mouse stencilled on the burning fuselage.

MR BISHOP'S PIG

The Swan was equipped with a pigsty; and one day Mr. Ned Bishop from 'Home Farm' delivered a baby pig to us; it was a 'runt' which would starve if left with the litter. We named him Horace and fed him with scraps until he was so large that I could ride on his back. We treated him as a pet and of course, he occasionally escaped and ran through the back door of the pub and out the front door, causing many pints to be spilled. Horace eventually went and was followed by a Harry and a Henry.

Mr. Bishop was often in the pub and one day, as I was practicing the piano, he asked me what I had done at school that day and when I said "Physics", he said "Are you sick then, boy?"

LIZZY AND LEAH FROM THE COTTAGES

On the opposite side of the road were two rows of terraced cottages. Ted Cook's wife, Lizzy, helped my mother on a part-time basis for many years. Another resident was Leah Harrowell, a widow who lived alone and whose favourite tipple was mild ale, or bitter beer. She always collected it in her own glass tankard, which was never washed. It was rumoured that she was from a wealthy family.

WITNESSING THE EVACUATED WOUNDED SOLDIERS

I distinctly remember walking, with my sister Phyllis, through the many elm trees in the meadow opposite The Swan, to the railway embankment. We had noticed that passenger trains were travelling north very slowly, one after the other. When we got close we could see soldiers crowded at the windows; some waved to us and many had blood-stained bandages. They had evacuated from Dunkirk and were being ferried away from London, to Northern hospitals.

BRISTOL BLENHEIM AEROPLANE CRASH

My Father worked part-time at RAF Halton, as a civilian clerk, travelling in the car of our neighbour, Mr Beasley, who was a Special Constable. On their return home one evening, they passed over Cooks Wharf Bridge, heading for Seabrook turn, when a Bristol Blenheim aeroplane crashed through the hedge in front of the car. One landing wheel went into the ditch which spun the aircraft round to straddle the road. It tipped onto its nose, the tail-plane rose up and hovered above the car but luckily balanced at that level, high above them.

The pilot had made such a skillful landing that the aircraft was deemed to be salvageable and a team of RAF fitters towed it back into South Field and prepared to make it airworthy again. They arrived every day for nearly a month and my brother Ray, and I, visited them every day where we were given jam sandwiches from their plentiful rations. When suitably airworthy an aircrew arrived and dozens of villagers watched anxiously as it took off using the full length of the field to reach sufficient airspeed.

BRITISH ARMY INVADES CHEDDINGTON

One morning, I looked out of the bedroom window to see an amazing sight - the British army had invaded the village. In our front drive was a radio communication vehicle. In Bob Whitehead's front gate was an anti-tank howitzer and the meadow, opposite was crawling with troops, tents, vehicles and armed men. A sentry with rifle was on guard to keep out civilians but he had no chance of preventing me and several other boys from slipping past when he was not looking.

Once again we were made welcome and offered goodies, but we were really interested in the guns and vehicles. An informal demonstration was given. Amongst the dramatic activity all around the site, one of the soldiers let off a 'Thunderflash' for our benefit. Health & Safety was unheard of!

During the week, Raymond and I were walking near the lynchet behind The Swan when a Churchill tank came crashing through a hedge toward us. It stopped, and the turret hatch was opened by a dirty faced gunner who asked us where he could get some milk. We were too excited to reply; we would have enlisted if we had been older! Then, some time later, with their training manoeuvres over, they were all gone; and the invasion of Normandy was still a long way off.

THE AMERICAN EIGHTH ARMY AIR FORCE ARRIVES

The appearance of the American Eighth Army Air Force, soon after 1942, was heralded by the arrival of convoys of khaki US trucks driven at high speed around the country roads. We had never seen so many vehicles before - and they were driven by black men. We soon began to meet the 'Yanks' as they wanted to try English warm beer in a quaint English pub.

One airman, Master Sergeant Johnny Samarin from Ohio, became a friend of the family and married a WAAF named Jean Burgess. My mother produced a wedding breakfast for them in The Swan and later he showed her how to make pumpkin pie. Mum offered them tea with strawberry jam and Jean stopped him from using a week's ration on one slice.

D-DAY: BOMBERS AND GLIDERS LEAVE CHEDDINGTON

The Allies began to win the war and the danger for the civilian population decreased, but for many servicemen there was worse to come as D-Day arrived. All the customers came out into the yard as an enormous cloud of bombers and gliders passed overhead on their way to help with the liberation of Europe. As the advance progressed Doug Wibden was repatriated from an enemy prisoner of war camp; and his return signalled the beginning of the end of our war, and the church bells could be rung again, in gratitude for the sacrifices of those who would not be returning to Cheddington.

Extract from the Leighton Buzzard Observer, 28th January, 1941

200 YEARS RECORD BROKEN

The Aylesbury Brewery Co. had asked the Council to permit hand flushing in the urinal at the Swan, Cheddington, to continue as the place is open to the sky and the risk of freezing any flushing apparatus was considerable. Mr. Seabrook asked why they need alter things. The place had been like that for 200 years.

The Chairman: The by-laws require a proper flushing apparatus to be put in, and we cannot allow the present conditions to remain without altering the bylaws. The Council's decision is to be enforced.

Mr and Mrs Castle of The Old Swan with Ray and Alan Castle behind

Mrs Castle (Old Swan), Arthur Edward (Ned) Bishop and Mrs Towell (housekeeper)

Mr and Mrs Castle with relatives, friends and guests

John Shand Kydd

BY HIS BROTHER BILL SHAND KYDD

EDUCATED AT STOWE
John was Frances and Norman Shand Kydd's eldest son and was educated, such as it was, at Stowe, the precursor of a legion of further Stoics starting with myself and followed by Peter's eldest son. John left early in order to join the war which he chose to do in the RAF.

KILLED IN A HARVARD TRAINER
John was flying in a Harvard trainer and decided to fly over Horton Hall. My other brother, Peter, my mother and myself were having lunch at the time and we all rushed out onto the lawn to wave our napkins at him.

He was obviously distracted by this and did not pay attention to his air speed. The Harvard was well known for having a very high stall speed, as a result he crashed in a field just close to Horton and was killed instantly.

POPULAR WITH FELLOW PILOTS
He was widely liked and very popular with his fellow pilots, one of whom I happened to meet when I was riding at Stratford races. He promised to send me John's flying boots, but they never appeared and I had no record of his name or his address.

Extract from The Leighton Buzzard Observer 11ᵗʰ November 1942

DEATH OF MR. J. V.W. SHAND KYDD

The death has occurred from an accident of L.A.C. John Victor William Shand Kydd (18) eldest son of Lt Col. and Mrs Shand Kydd of Horton Hall. He was educated at Fernden School, Haslemere and Stowe School Buckingham and was an aircraft student. Lt. Col. Shand Kydd has lived in this district for about two years having taken over Horton Hall from Capt. Strettell.

The funeral took place at St. Giles Church on Saturday. The Rev W.T. Rees conducted the service. The mourners included Lt Col. N Shand Kydd (father), Mrs Shand Kydd (stepmother), Mr Peter Shand Kydd (brother), Miss P Shand Kydd (sister). The church was crowded with members of the RAF Home Guard and Women's British Legion. Horton Home Guards acted as the bearers. The coffin was draped with the Union Jack and a bugle sounded the Reveille and Last Post. Mr. A. Fathers was organist. There were beautiful floral tributes.

On Sunday morning at St. Giles Church the Rev. W.T. Rees spoke highly of the young life that had been lost.

The grave of LAC John Shand Kydd who was killed on September 10th 1941 whilst flying over Horton

The grave of William John Wesley, a Gunner in the Royal Artillery. He died aged 31 on 11th March, 1944.

Mary Richardson

GRAYS, ESSEX

SCHOOL

I was ten when war broke out and I attended a preparatory school near Grays in Essex. The attached secondary school took boarders and was a grammar school.

In September 1939 the preparatory school and grammar school were closed because it was to be used for housing Dutch refugees. The Dutch children marvelled at the sight of double decker buses as they had not seen them before. Once a week I collected work from school. After Christmas school reopened without boarders. I took the 11+ in June 1940 and passed to go to the grammar school. At this time children could leave school at 14.

THE BLITZ YEARS

Air raid shelters were built in the school grounds, approached by about 10 steps. Apart from the one for 5th and 6th years they were unlit and had benches (Health and safety rules today!!!). Teachers sitting at the base of the steps read to us from Dorothy Sayers books (Lord Peter Wimsey). We were in the shelters most days as German planes passed over on the way to London. It was very disruptive to my first year education – but we looked forward to the air raids!

NEIGHBOURS

We shared a front path with neighbours. The lady next door could hardly be called house proud. The back garden was approximately 50 feet long. At the bottom there was a shed with two nanny goats – these had to be taken each day to a field, and obviously chewed anything on the side of the path. People at the back complained to the council, but we were the only people who could complain because of the shared path. This was part of their ambition to move to a smallholding. Next to the goat shed was a large chicken run. Half way down the garden was another shed housing rabbits, indoors in the bath were ducks!! Underneath the stairs was stored bales of straw and sacks of animal feed. The garden was laid out with vegetables and a mature apple tree. When they moved to this smallholding they took the apple tree, strapped on the roof of a van – overhanging more than half of the road. The daughter of the house had to visit her sister for a bath, which was all right until a doodle bug damaged the sister's house.

VISITS TO MY RELATIVES

Every citizen was issued with an Identity card. We lived in a military sensitive area so there was access to residents only. I had an aunt who had a pub cum small holding near Maidstone and the police gave us permission to pass through the area. One day we watched dog fights overhead, and my uncle out in the field was targeted with a machine gun. My uncle kept cows and chickens and pigs so we had plenty of milk and eggs. They made their own butter. A licence was required to kill a pig, so in return for a promise of pork, on a set day the inspector sent the constable on a road a long way off. We used to go to visit about twice a year for a good feed.

On going to visit my cousin near Chatham, we were turned back as we got off the bus. This meant going back one stop and walking across the fields. On returning from these visits we crossed the Thames by ferry and then caught a bus from Tilbury. About 500 yards up the road police boarded the bus and removed people without the correct identity cards.

We kept chickens in the back garden as did our neighbours. At harvest time the children gleaned dropped ears of corn after the sheaves had been removed. This helped with chicken food, as we surrendered all but one of our egg ration coupons for chicken food. We also had an inter-form competition at school to see who could gather the greatest weight of wild rosehips. These were used to manufacture rose hip syrup.

WEAPONS

Before the doodlebugs, the Germans dropped butterfly bombs. These were yellow cylinders about the size of cocoa tins and had yellow wings. Police toured the area warning us not to touch them as they would explode on being picked up. When there were warnings of the approach of doodle bugs we had to retire to the school shelters. More stories read to us!! A couple of V2s fell in Tilbury, fired from Holland. All you heard was a bang and a whistle – no warning. They caused a lot of damage – all the windows of the ferry boats. The parachute descending towards the village was shot down by anti-aircraft fire, so it exploded in the air.

EVACUATED

One girl, daughter of the Dock's Superintendent, was evacuated to Canada for the duration of the war.

SOCIAL CLASS

My father was in the Firewatch Group. My friend's father was an officer in the Home Guard. She used to come into school and say "My father had the Polish officers round last night." She would stand at the bus stop with her National Savings book in her hand and show it off. We all lived in council houses, we were in the smaller ones, she in the bigger ones at the other end of the road.

I was 16 when the war in Europe ended.

Jim Richardson

THE BLITZ

To me, the London Blitz began on September 7th, 1940 and ended May 10th, 1941. These dates are firmly imprinted upon my mind. I lived in South West Ham. The area is now part of Newham. The Royal Docks, Victoria, Albert and King George Vth, were only a mile away. These, and the associated factories, were to be targets for attack in due course.

SEPTEMBER 7TH

September 7th is a date etched in my memory and also into all East End Londoners alive at that time. I was sixteen.

I was to be busy with the Scouts, collecting paper and cardboard as usual. I told my mother that (if a raid happened) I would take shelter in the shelter behind the church, from where I could watch and see what happened. Sure enough, the warning sounded and, with my Scout friends, I moved into the shelter. The shelter had four bays running north to south. Two bays had entrances at the north and two at the south. We moved to one of the south entrances, which we thought would enable us to see any aircraft passing from east to west along the line of the Thames.

In due course half a dozen German aircraft appeared, were fired at, were not hit and passed away to the west, as on the previous two weeks.

When all was quiet we went out into the street to see if any shrapnel, pieces of anti aircraft shell, had fallen. We were young and rather excited, and hoped to see signs of what had happened. Unfortunately we did not, but later would do. We expected the "all clear" to sound, but it did not. Instead the guns started to fire again.

Back to the south end of the shelter, we stood in the entrance and looked to the east. It was frightening; the sky was black with aircraft. I think they were two abreast, and the queue disappeared into the distance and, slightly behind and to the south of the first column, was another one. German records are said to show that there were 300 bombers in this formation, and I believe it.

This bomber formation passed by. We heard the sound of falling bombs and heard the explosions. We were not able to see the point of impact, about a mile away with houses in between. We saw black smoke rising and turning to flames. This all happened in no more than ten minutes. Occasionally we heard a nearer bomb falling, and moved into the shelter before returning to look out from the entrance. Finally all the aircraft had moved away, leaving dense smoke and flames rising from the direction of the river. The "all clear" sounded, we cleared away what we had been doing and I dashed home to show that I was ok.

I then hurried up to look over the Sewer banks at Silvertown and the docks. From end to end it was a mass of fire and smoke. Looking further to the west beyond Silvertown, we could see more smoke and flame from further up the river. Silvertown is a narrow strip of land between the Thames and the Royal Docks. It was full of factories of various kinds, and dockside warehouses, and many small houses occupied by families who work in the factories and the docks.

My brother, Albert, had been working on the allotment as this raid began. He, and other allotment holders, in a shelter, had an unobstructed view of the destruction and was in quite a state of shock as a result.

No sooner had it got dark when the alarm sounded again, and we returned to our Anderson Shelter. Then all night long we heard aircraft approaching from the east. The first one passed over and as it passed it dropped bombs. We heard them scream and explode, and the aircraft moved on, its noise passing away to the west. As its sound died away, we heard the next one approaching from the east, and so it went on and on. We could see the glow from the fires, and overhead we could see the underside of the barrage balloon, glowing orange and red from the fires.

There was no response from our ant-aircraft batteries. Searchlights were certainly probing the sky but no aircraft were illuminated.

Luckily no bombs fell close enough to cause us damage. The bombs were falling in areas close to the docks, and as far as West Ham was concerned, Custom House, Canning Town, Tidal Basin and Silvertown were suffering the damage. The Ministry of Information communiqué next morning spoke of a severe attack with damage and approximately 400 dead. Silvertown was more or less completely evacuated leaving it to the firemen, police and First Aid Rescue units.

To complete the evacuation, some people were taken by boat across the river to the Kent side but all were out at the finish.

They were taken well away from the area, and it was some time before any were allowed back. The fires continued to burn for several days. There was flour, sugar, rubber, tar, vegetable oil, fuel oil and various other chemicals in the mixture.

German bombers over London, 5.05 p.m., September 7th, 1940. The Battle of Britain was at its height and London was adjusting to the shock of the Luftwaffe's assault on the capital. Londoners soon learned to recognise the Dorniers and Heinkels that came over in their hundreds until their power was smashed by 'The Few'. This picture, taken from the attacking bombers, is now in the possession of the RAF. It is of the local area where Jim Richardson and his family lived at the time. [Actually just below the top edge, one-ninth in]. The large oval track between the two planes was West Ham Stadium, now built over. The two large roads under the right-hand bomber are the Beckton Road [the straight one] and the present A137 [the curved one].

MY WAR SERVICE BEGINS

From July 2nd 1942, anyone joining the British Army found themselves entering a depot of the General Service Corps for a period of six weeks.

During this time there was square-bashing, p.ed., general infantry training including firing a rifle and a Bren gun, as well as a series of tests, both intelligence and practical. It was hoped that by doing this it would enable recruits to be given jobs which would be suitable to them. There should be no more square pegs in round holes.

On July 2nd I joined the No 1 Depot of the General Service Corps at Crookham, Hampshire. This was a Depot and Training Centre of the RAMC (The Royal Army Medical Corps) and the General Service Corps had taken over half of it. There were similar depots in other parts of the country.

At the end of this six weeks I was deemed suitable to be trained as a Radio Mechanic and this seemed fine to me.

ROYAL CORPS OF SIGNALS: PRESTATYN

As a result I was posted to the Royal Corps of Signals at Prestatyn in North Wales. Here the Signals had taken over a Holiday Camp. I was the only recruit from Crookham sent to Prestatyn.

I got off the train at Prestatyn to find another twenty or thirty lads, all joining the Signals.

We did not go to the Holiday camp. We were marched off into the town and put into an empty house, under the charge of a junior NCO, where we slept on the floor. Next morning we found that there were a hundred or so of us altogether, occupying four or five empty houses.

I stayed here for three weeks, doing PE on the sand dunes every morning, and then a group of us, thirty or so, were taken by train to Huddersfield where we joined the Signal Trade Training Battalion.

Here we slept on double tier bunks, in buildings that at one time had been a woollen mill. The Signals were scattered in a number of such like mills — cookhouse and NAAFI in two others. The library had been taken over as a training school. I was given a rifle and had to sit a maths test. Anyone who failed maths had extra maths instruction for an evening.

The first week here was spent doing fatigues. In the second week the radio course began. On the third day two of us were called to the office and told that we were posted to the Medical Corps at Crookham with the recommendation that we be trained as Laboratory Assistants.

MEDICAL CORPS: CROOKHAM

So — back to Crookham. Here I found some ten of, us all from the July 2nd Call-Up. Some were from Signals, some from Armoured Corps, others from Infantry. All had been Laboratory Assistants before Call-Up and here we were to be trained as Lab. Assistants in RAMC.

We were all interviewed by the Pathologist from Command Laboratory which was part of the Military Hospital at Aldershot. We were told it was to be Laboratory Assistants or Nursing Orderlies, so we had little choice.

There followed six weeks basic RAMC training: more square bashing, more PE, First Aid, bandages, splints, stretcher carrying and bed making. At the end of six weeks I was posted, with two others, to the Command Laboratory at a Military Hospital a few miles from Chester.

COMMAND LABORATORY, MILITARY HOSPITAL: CHESTER

This was a standard Military Hospital, similar in size and appearance to the original Stoke Mandeville Hospital near here. The laboratory was in what would otherwise have been a hospital ward.

The pathologist in charge was a colonel, Irish, and very pleasant and friendly and there was also a lieutenant, a younger pathologist who was very pleasant. Apart from these there was a sergeant, a Regular soldier, who had served in India. There were also two trained laboratory assistants. When we arrived there was already the remnants of a previous course.

Our training course started at once. It was interesting enough: simple bacteriology, bio-chemical testing, blood sugar, blood urea, urine urea etc., blood counts, blood grouping and so on. We were soon involved in helping with the day-to-day work of the laboratory.

Pathologists carry out post-mortem examinations and, before long we were taken to see our first. The pathologist said he needed three men to help him: one to help with the actual performance, one to take his dictated notes and one to keep his pipe filled and lit!

One of the experienced assistants put on his gown and gloves and took the practical part. My job was to take his notes.

At this time I had not seen a dead body and was rather worried about how I would behave. There were a number of people watching, and they all seemed to take it as a matter of course, and so did I. When it was finished we all went off to dinner. It was not long before it was my turn to wear gown and gloves and play an active part in the performance.

At the end of three months I passed the examination and was graded as Laboratory Assistant, Grade Three.

CHARTHAM
Then posted to a small Military Hospital at Chartham, a few miles from Canterbury, Kent. It was a small hospital in what had been a Mental Hospital. Very comfortable. The laboratory consisted of a captain, a corporal and I made up the second assistant. Just the normal run of a medium sized Military Hospital – fairly busy and interesting work. Unfortunately this did not last. After five weeks I was sent home on Embarkation leave.

PREPARATION FOR OVERSEAS DRAFT
After fourteen days at home I had to report to the RAMC depot at Leeds, on May 10th, 1943, to join overseas draft RCGKW. No indication, of course, about the final destination.

There were three of us sent from the hospital at Chartham; one to the same draft as me and the third to another.

A large number of men reported to Leeds on this day. On arrival we were separated into our appropriate drafts and taken by truck to our temporary accommodation. For me this was a large, empty house some ten minutes walk from the depot. Here we slept on the floor, being marched to the depot for meals.

There followed four days of rushing around as we were given tropical kit. At this time, tropical kit for the army was khaki drill shorts and shirts for daytime wear, long trousers for after dark, hose tops and gaiters for the legs. This was all issued to us in a rush together with a topee (a sun hat; not a true pith helmet). We were also given a smaller, white sea kit bag to take on the boat with a list of what we should pack, while our other kit bag would go separately by sea. We had to paint our details on both kit bags – name, number, RAMC, draft letters and destination code 'A'.

We did not know where we were going although it was obviously tropical. There were several possibilities in the Middle East e.g. Persia, Iraq.

Our standard kit bags were taken away some time on May 14th. It was my twentieth birthday! At ten o'clock that evening we were marched to the tram terminal, loaded up with our kit. I am not sure whether we had tin hats. We did have our greatcoats.

The local people knew we were going. As we marched in the darkness, doors opened and people called out "Good luck!"

There was small crowd of people at the tram stop. I remember a couple of elderly people in tears and a rather drunk ATS girl passing round a bag of chips.

There was our special train at the station and men from the depot to see us on our train.

"Plenty of room."

" Six to a carriage."

" Take off your boots."

" Make yourself comfortable."

The train pulled away. It was dark: blackout.

Some who knew the area tried to make out which way we were going. I think we all slept.

As it began to get light the next morning we awoke and again, tried to see where we were.

Finally the train slowed to walking pace and we passed a group of railway workers who said we were approaching Avonmouth. The train stopped alongside our troopship 'SS Mataroa'.

SS MATAROA

We gathered our kit, left the train and climbed up the gangway, at the top of which a couple of military policemen helped us on board. It was to be five weeks before we walked on dry land again. We were taken below to our mess deck. Members of the crew were aboard. They told us where we were going: first to Durban, South Africa and from there, by another ship, to India. Of course we were unable to let our families know where we were going. There were no telephones and any letters had to pass the censor. It would be twelve weeks before our people would know where we had finished up.

The fall of France and the entry of Italy into the war in June 1940 meant that we were unable to send ships through the Mediterranean Sea, and so all supplies to the Middle East, South East Asia and the Far East had to go round the Cape of Good Hope. Although in the early days one ship had made the full journey it was found better to build transit camps at Durban, South Africa, and to disembark there. The ships used for this part of the journey then sailed to America, either south or north, and took supplies and food from there back to England, and the cycle then continued. Men were held in the transit camps then went by other ships to finish the journey.

Meanwhile, at Avonmouth, more trains arrived during the day so that, by late afternoon, the ship was apparently full.

MESS DECK ACCOMMODATION

Mess Deck accommodation meant that we lived slept and ate in the same place. Long tables were bolted to the floor with benches on either side for seating. Hammock hooks on girders overhead gave us sleeping arrangements. There were a couple of hundred soldiers on our mess deck. We were the first deck down and there were stairs from the surface deck down to us and another set to the deck below. We did have portholes on our deck and, later on the voyage we were allowed to have one open. Those below had no such luxury. We were at the after end of the ship; that is, behind the engine room. Beyond us was yet another set of men's decks. A closable, watertight door separated the two sets. This was open during the day, with a guard there to close it in the event of an alarm. There was a similar two level men's deck at the front end of the ship.

OCCUPATIONS OF THE DRAFT

There must have been somewhere to stow our sea kit bags, but I am afraid I can't remember. There was a bank of coat hooks to hang our greatcoats. Our draft consisted of about sixty men of mixed RAMC trades. There were two other newly qualified laboratory assistants. We had met before when we were transferred from other units back in September the previous year. The draft also included five newly qualified pharmacists. These, as was customary, were all sergeants. There were a couple of older sergeants, presumably responsible for discipline and good order. There were also three or four corporals. The rest were plain privates. There were three young officers in charge, all doctors I suppose. We only saw them on pay parade. The officers on board all slept in cabins. They probably had extra bunk fitted, but were more comfortable than us. They also ate in the officer's mess, but more about that later. Washbasins, for us, were in rows on the open well deck.

SLEEPING ARRANGEMENTS

That night we settled down in our hammocks. These were numbered so that we always had the same one. There were enough but there were not enough hammock hooks and so some slept on the mess tables, or under the tables, or between the tables although later in the voyage there was the opportunity to sleep on deck.

A hammock is very comfortable to sleep in. We needed to step on a mess table, open the hammock and climb in. The side of the hammock wraps around you so there is no risk of slipping out.

LIFE ON A TROOP SHIP

When we awoke the next morning we were steaming north in the Irish Sea, the ship towing a barrage ball to deter possible enemy aircraft. We began getting used to life on a troop ship - always carry your life jacket, keep your water bottle full of water. We were given a small tin of Emergency Rations. It contained, we were told, four ounces of chocolate – fortified with vitamins and minerals. This was to be our lifesaver, together with our water, in the event of finishing up in a lifeboat, or, worse, on a raft. No smoking below deck. At this time most men smoked. No smoking on deck after dark. Boat station every morning while the ship was inspected by the ship's captain and the senior service man.

Each ship had a nucleus of military personnel that travelled with the ship. There was always an officer major, say, very often a survivor of World War 1, a sergeant major, a few medical personnel and service personnel. Passengers were usually raked in to supplement. Our boat station was a stack of rafts secured on the well deck.

PE on the boat deck in batches every afternoon. This gave us a chance to see all the boat's armament. There was a six-inch gun at the back, and a Bofors gun. Around the boat deck Oerlikon guns and machine guns and a rocket launcher. Crew-members were capable of using these guns. There was also a small number of army gunners and marines to man this armament. They remained with the boat until it returned to England.

At the end of the first day we passed between the guard ships controlling the boom defences and entered the Firth of Clyde where the ship anchored. This then gave us the last chance to write letters before we were to sail. We now began to realise what life on a troop ship involved.

We kept army hours: reveille at 6a.m., lights out at 10.15p.m., fresh water on tap for washing and shaving two hours morning and evening, queuing for your turn, no possibility of washing clothes. Warm seawater showers were available. We were given a tablet of seawater soap, so called. It gave a layer of slime over the body. There was a large tank of drinking water on the mess deck. Someone had to top this up while fresh water was available.

OFFICER CADET CORPS MEMBERS

I don't know how many men were on the ship – perhaps three hundred or so. Quite a mixture. These were us, RAMC, some Signals, some Engineers, a fairly large group from the Armoured Corps and a small group of sailors. In particular there was a group, say thirty, who were Officer Cadet Corps members. They at least knew where they were going – to India to be commissioned into the Indian Army. They were all being commissioned from the ranks and were completing their training on the way. All officers in the Indian Army were obliged to pass an Army Examination in Elementary Urdu and this language class was on the boat. There was a large cabin as their classroom, and their cabin could be used by others when the OCTU did not need it. The cabin contained a piano and sometimes there was singing or other entertainment organised there, but not after nightfall. Noise travels a long way over sea and U-boats had been known to locate convoys by following noise. I remember two concerts arranged on the boat – a quite good one by the Armoured Corps Draft and another by OCTU. They had a talented violinist who had brought his violin along with him. He had been Leader of a BBC orchestra and he gave two performances.

FATIGUES

Troopship fatigues were given out – duties that needed to be done regularly. I think that all of the RAMC Draft were involved, except those who looked after the mess deck - kept it clean, collected and distributed food etc. Some of our draft worked in the sickbay, some waited in the officer's mess and washed and wiped up their china and cutlery, two peeled potatoes for the officer's mess and one worked helping the ship's baker. I found myself working, helping the crew stewards, in what was called the utensil store. This involved giving out cleaning materials, soap, soda, scrubbing brushes and cleaning swabs to those involved in cleaning duties in the ship, and, in the early days of the voyage, collecting spare lifejackets and stowing them below in the ship. Certain jobs also went to members of other drafts. The decks had to be washed down with seawater early every morning before reveille and some must have been involved in cleaning toilets etc.

THE ALARM PROCEDURE

For those not involved in fatigues there were guards or sentries to be posted. Someone had to be at every waterproof door to close it if an alarm was sounded, and some were needed to keep people moving along passages or stairways to stop them being impeded.

We had to learn the alarm signals:

A continuous ring was for submarines. (You get on deck to one of the 10 boat stations.)

A series of short rings meant aircraft. (You get below deck to dodge being machine-gunned.)

FOOD ON SHIP

Food on the ship was quite reasonable – three meals a day. There was freshly baked bread. There was porridge for breakfast, of course. There were sausages and bacon (It was a meat ship so there was plenty of cold-storage.) plus other meat in stews. There was tinned meat, corned beef and Spam and baked beans of course. No one went hungry. Potatoes were washed but boiled in their skins. We had friends working in the officer's mess. They of course, (our friends) ate rather well and half a roast chicken sometimes appeared in our mess deck of an evening.

JOINING THE CONVOY

We stayed at anchor in the Clyde for a day and then, in the late afternoon, went through the boom defences and, before it got dark, we could see in the distance the coast of Northern Ireland to the left of the ship as we were sailing roughly westward.

Next morning there was no land in sight. We were now in convoy, able to see ships spread out around us and, in the far distance, the escorting convoys - the pattern of ships around us changing and reforming as the convoy zigzagged its way along, and this pattern was to continue day after day.

We had been advised that for the first three nights we should sleep fully dressed. For at least three days we convoyed to the west and then turned south. Presumably by now we had given enough distance to the French Atlantic Coast.

WARMER CLIMES

Then one day the ship's stewards appeared wearing white uniforms, and the weather was somewhat warmer, and we began to see flying fish disturbed by the boat.

After, I think, twelve days we were told that on the following day water would be on tap all day for clothes washing, and the crew told us that on the day after we would arrive at Freetown, West Africa.

So clothes washing went ahead and we all had a change of shirt and underwear but no chance of a fresh water shower. We were, in fact, denied this luxury for five weeks.

During these two weeks of our voyage we had seen, for a few days, a cruiser in the escort and also an aircraft carrier.

FREETOWN: WEST AFRICA

On the morning of our fourteenth day palm trees began to appear over the horizon and in due course we anchored in the river at Freetown.

Soon local Africans came out, mainly by paddling canoes, to try and sell us bananas or oranges. They wanted to throw up a rope. If money were dropped to them they would put fruit in a basket for us to pull up. We had been told not to buy from them and guards, on duty to check, would throw off the ropes although, in time, some did manage to acquire fruit. More commonly young lads on the canoes would ask to have money thrown into the sea, when they would dive in and retrieve it.

Roughly a dozen men on our mess deck got off here. I think they were engineers due to spend one eighteen-month spell in Freetown. West African climate and diseases were thought so bad that eighteen months was thought to be enough for any man to bear. At least they knew when they would return home. We did not.

There was, of course, a severe risk of malaria here and we had no mosquito nets. Instead we were given jelly containing Citronella, the odour of which either discouraged or confused the mosquito. So this we applied and hoped. We spent two nights at Freetown and certainly nobody on our draft developed malaria during the rest of our journey.

We sailed from Freetown at six o'clock on the second morning and soon land had disappeared from view. The journey continued as before. We were regularly seeing flying fish now and some men developed sunburn. All days were similar now. The only news of the war we received was from a news sheet typed and pinned up on the notice board on our deck.

Members of the draft organised a sweep on the 1943 Derby and I drew the winner.

CAPE TOWN: SOUTH AFRICA

After a further fourteen days we arrived in Cape Town. The day before we had water for washing clothes. We just spent one night here - enough to stock up with fresh water.

DURBAN: SOUTH AFRICA

The convoy sailed, still zigzagging, and land disappeared again. We obviously rounded the Cape of Good Hope and travelled northwards, reaching Durban after six or seven days. We arrived off the port one afternoon, but had to spend time going up and down the coast before entering port next morning and tying up at the dockside.

THE LADY IN WHITE

The engines shut down and we could hear a lady singing. She was standing on a box and was dressed in a long white frock, wore a red hat and was singing into a megaphone. She sang patriotic songs and songs that were popular in war time Britain. She went along the dock singing to every ship in turn. This was 'The Lady in White', Perla Siedle. She was a retired professional singer. She sang to welcome every troop convoy into Durban from its start in August 1940 until the convoys were able to use the Mediterranean Sea once more in late 1943. She sang them all out again. We loved and appreciated it.

TRANSIT CAMP IN CLAIRWOOD

We had been five weeks on that boat and were happy to be on land once more. From the dockside we went by train (about forty minutes for the journey) to the Transit Camp at a place called Clairwood. It was the site of a horse-racing track. There were, in fact, two camps: one for the army and one for the RAF. We did not see the RAF camp but I imagine it was much the same as ours. The army camp consisted of a series of large, rather open, brick bungalows. They had walls up to about windowsill height, with brick pillars to support a tiled roof. They were weatherproof and, because of the climate, quite habitable. The floors were of concrete. We must have been given palliasses because I can remember breaking open two bales of straw to share between us. A concrete floor can be quite comfortable when you are tired. Our draft occupied two of these bungalows. We called them cowsheds. Officers occupied a similar structure but they were six to one of them, and they had camp beds and folding chairs and tables.

Once settled in the first job was to shower. We had not been able to shower for five weeks. We probably smelled, but we were all the same. There was a big block of hand basins in the open, and a big block of showers. We also needed to wash our clothes. We were to wear our normal English battledress. It was not hot enough for tropical.

We were able to send letters home from here, but not able to say where we were or where we were going. Our letters were still censored. There was no mail for us, of course. Our families only had our draft reference as address and we were not to get these until India.

ADVICE ON BEHAVIOUR IN DURBAN

However, on arrival we were given a folded information leaflet, 'Welcome to Durban', similar to those you can pick up in an English town tourist office. This included a map of Durban with places of interest marked: churches, canteens, cinemas etc. plus information on trains, buses etc. plus information and advice about behaviour and local problems. South Africa, at this time, had a colour problem. There were the European types, mainly of British and Dutch descent, then the local race, mainly Zulu, plus a sizeable Indian population. The Zulus and Indians did the menial tasks. We found it embarrassing to see them step off the pavement to give us room to pass. On buses they had the back seats at the top of the bus, and if there were not enough seats they had to get up for us. We were advised to be careful about this.

A CABLEGRAM HOME

We were able to send a Forces cablegram home from here, not that it was much use to us. You could send a choice of three phrases from a given list. There was no phrase that said we were still in transit or only half way. The best was to say that we were fit and well. That, I think, cost something like five shillings about twenty-five pence in today's money. Rather better, we could address and stamp an empty envelope in the tourist office; they would put a copy of 'Welcome to Durban' in and post it. It went by sea mail and arrived home after we had left Durban so at least our families would know where we had been.

FITNESS TRAINING

At the camp we had PE or similar activities in the morning, jogging, rope climbing, football – we had no football boots so played in army boots. We also had a rugby match in army boots. There was also an assault course. There was a group of Army Physical Training instructors in the camp. I think the idea was to keep us occupied and reasonably fit while there. Food here was very good. I particular remember meeting large tins of tomato jam – very nice.

LEISURE TIME

After dinner our time was our own. We went into Durban by train. I can't remember if there was a fare or not. However, we had to leave guards to safeguard our belongings, as the 'cattle sheds' were completely open. We even had to have a rota doing two-hour shifts during the night. Even worse, we had to guard the officers' quarters while they were out, although occasionally, with six officers per bungalow, one or two of them might stay in and so we would not be needed.

The first day we were not allowed to leave camp. The second day Durban was invaded and we explored it. First stop was usually the Methodist church where there was a cup of tea and a cake, free. Then there was the Services canteen. Here, if it was busy, you were let in once there was room, then you took a tray and helped yourself, paying at the end.

After three years of rationing at home, the food here was remarkable. We did not go hungry at home, but here was everything that had disappeared from English food: plenty of meat, oranges, bananas, grapes, real cream and ice-cream. At times when this canteen was not so busy you sat down and they gave you waitress service.

There was also a golf club and a Jewish club where they filled large tables of ten or so seats and then gave waitress service.

In time we got to visit cinemas and there were also Public Houses. Cape Brandy was quite potent and cheap. I seem to remember that opening hours were rather short. After five weeks at sea, by mid evening there were quite a few alcoholic soldiers or airmen in the town. Still, we did look after our mates and get them back to the station, and the camp, safely. Very often the luggage racks in the carriages were filled with rather tipsy men. After the first night the number of alcoholics did seem to decrease.

It was not unusual for small groups of men, say two or three, being invited into a Durban house for the evening. I went around in a group of six, rather too many, so did not have this pleasure.

We did have two full days out from the camp. On one we marched some five miles to the coast, took a picnic lunch and some of us managed to paddle in the sea. The second time we were taken by truck about ten miles to another part of the coast, where we attempted rope bridging. Some fell in the sea and then we marched back to the camp.

Yes, we certainly enjoyed our five weeks in Durban. Then came our last evening out. The boats were due in. This was the time for another excess of alcoholism. By nine o'clock people were busy shepherding their friends back to the station. The Marines had taken a large trolley from the station and were busy collecting their mates from the pavement.

The last night we were confined to camp, and the next day, back on the train to the dockyard. We had arrived in Durban in early July and this was now mid August.

DEPARTING DURBAN

There were two P&O liners waiting for us, painted grey of course. The RAF boarded the 'Stratheden'. The 'Strathmore' was for the Army, some Marines, a small group of sailors and about forty Americans. Where they came from I don't know. I did not see any of the OCTU.

The Lady in White was there singing to us and when we sailed she was on the far end of the breakwater singing Auld Lang Syne – a very moving experience.

There were just the two ships in the convoy, escorted by a British Cruiser and our Australian destroyers. Once more we lived, ate, slept on Mess decks. Food was reasonable.

We were well beyond the limit of possible air attack, but German and Japanese submarines were still a possibility, and so the convoy zigzagged. We carried life jackets, water bottles and emergency rations and the ship was darkened at night.

Our boat station, this time, was on the boat deck and we, in fact, had a lifeboat although there were plenty of life rafts about the ship.

I found myself allocated to a First Aid party. We were not needed although during a couple of morning boat stations we were told to collect 'a victim' (a poor member of the crew) from somewhere on the boat, strap him into a special stretcher, carry him to a boat station, leaving him there after instructing whoever was in charge there, to make sure they took him onto the lifeboat with them.

The journey went off without incident, although I did find myself, with one other, watching over a genuine patient in isolation for one night. He was suspected of having meningitis. Luckily he did not.

DEOLALI, NEAR BOMBAY: INDIA

After fourteen days we docked in Bombay. So far we had been using British or British type currency-

pounds, shillings and pence. South African currency was shaped and looked like the British and both were used together. Only the pound notes had different colours. Now we had to change to, and get used to, rupees and annas. Sixteen annas make one rupee. There were also smaller units, pies and pice. So all our currency was collected and changed for Indian on the boat, and then redistributed to us appropriately.

We were soon off the boat, on to a train and, in a couple of hours of slow journey, arrived at Deolali, a large military area, and were delivered to the RAMC depot there. Here we were reunited with our kit bags, last seen at Leeds, thirteen weeks before. We had left Leeds on May 14th and arrived at Deolali August 19th.

SENDING MAIL HOME

Waiting for us at Deolali was a large volume of mail from England. We were now able to write home giving our actual address – RAMC, Deolali, India Command. All our mail home had to be censored of course.

There were, in fact, three ways to send mail. The first was ordinary sea mail. This would take about eight weeks to get home. It was all right for lengthy items that were not very urgent. Not all was to arrive. I can't remember the cost of sea mail.

Then there was the air graph: a blank form, about octavo size, of fairly stout paper, had a box at the top, for the address. The remainder was marked out as an area of correspondence. This was written on, a four anna stamp applied and handed in for the censor. This was then photographed onto a reel of microfilm. The film was flown to England, developed, each item placed in an envelope and delivered by post. Fairly quick.

Then there was the air letter card, similar to the air letter cards you can buy to use here now. At this time we were issued with one of these a week. Postage, again, was four annas. This was sent by air.

All this mail was censored locally, that is, by an officer who knew you. There was also the Green Envelope Scheme. One a week was available and up to three letters could be placed in it, each stamped appropriately, and these would be taken to Base for censorship.

'LIFE' UNDER THE CANVAS

Here, in Deolali, we lived in large canvas marquees, about a dozen men in each. We had wooden frame beds. These beds were fairly common in army use. They were of the type known as charpoys: a rectangular frame of fairly stout wood, smoothed, with thick string stretched along and across the frame, and interlocked to give two or three inch mesh which supported bedding and, of course, the sleeper. They were, in fact, quite comfortable to sleep on. They did have a drawback, they did harbour insects- notably bed bugs. You won't have met bed bugs – reddish-brown in colour, about the size of a ladybird and they bite and can cause an itchy bump. We were issued with mosquito nets and also cotton bed sheets.

In time bed bugs would migrate to the corners of the mosquito nets. They could easily be dealt with using an ordinary electric iron. If you had a metal bed, then a blowlamp was the cure. With a wooden bed frame the only cure (and this only temporary), was to wash the frame with disinfectant. We all became used to frequent de-bugging of beds.

AN INTRODUCTION TO OUR SERVICE IN INDIA

Now all our English battledress was taken away, and our greatcoats, our underwear etc. and given its first proper wash (Indian-style) for three months. We were now wearing full tropical kit.

We were, of course, welcomed by the major and sergeant major of the depot, who tried to explain what they could about Indians, Indian money and Indian shop keepers. We were taken out in a long crocodile, on a two or three hour walk, passing through two Indian villages to see for ourselves.

TRAIN JOURNEYS

We also had advice about train journeys. At that time there were very few express trains, if any. Trains travelled long distances slowly. It was not unusual to spend two or three days on the train, often on the same train. There were no buffet cars. Trains made long stops at stations with refreshment facilities for breakfast, lunch, and dinner. The train conductor rang ahead to say the number of meals required. You then stopped, ate your meal and the train then went off on its journey. There were prices fixed for a Forces meal, and after your journey you were reimbursed. The daily amount for the meals was about three rupees. (I hope my memory is correct.) An anna was approximately a penny (old money), a rupee one shilling and four pence so a day's food at fixed prices was about four shillings (twenty pence). Remember that at that time, as a simple Private, my pay was less than two pounds a week.

FOOD AT DEOLALI

At Deolali there was ample food but not of the quantity and quality we had enjoyed in Durban. There were eggs, there were scrawny chickens, plenty of bread, dehydrated potato (therefore mash), tinned meat – corned beef, Spam etc., and tinned sausages. The sausages were soya links; square in cross section, pleasant when you first met them but when you had them day after day, very boring. If you threw one into the air it would never fall back to the ground. Large birds, kites, would catch it first. In fact, if you walked across open ground carrying your dinner on a plate it was likely that a bird would knock it out of your hands. There was little fresh meat and it was tough. There was dehydrated meat, (mince). This was turned into rissoles. Tinned fish appeared as fishcakes. Anything that we did not eat would be taken by local Indians, waiting as we left the mess tent.

JOURNEY TO RAZMAK: NORTH WEST FRONTIER

After a week I was posted to the Combined Indian Military Hospital at Razmak. Where was Razmak? The North West Frontier bordering Afghanistan.

I had read Rudyard Kipling and thought that the frontier was a rough and wild place. I was posted to the military hospital at Peshawar for onward transmission to Razmak. I don't think the office at Deolali knew the procedure to get to Razmak. Peshawar, being in the North West Frontier province, would probably know the rest.

DEOLALI TO PESHAWAR

I was given a warrant for a railway ticket, and told to catch the Bombay to Peshawar train when it stopped at Deolali sometime around midnight. I was to have a companion for part of the journey; someone who had come from the same hospital at Chartham was being posted to Lahore. But I had almost another two days journey beyond.

There were three classes on Indian trains. Officers travelled first class, other ranks second class. Some well-to-do Indians would be found in the first or second, but the majority travelled third class which was rather primitive.

Second class carriages contained upholstered benches. Using the luggage racks a second-class carriage could sleep five people lying down – two on either side and, as the railway was broad gauge, one on a central bench. If there were more than five some had to sleep sitting down.

So the pair of us were taken, with all our luggage, to the station late at night to await the train. It was not particularly late arriving.

Tropical dress at this time was shorts during the daylight hours, long trousers after dark when the mosquitoes were active. However, whilst travelling it was always long trousers that were worn.

The train came to a halt, we found a second-class carriage, hammered on the door until it was opened and climbed in. I think there was room for us to lie down, and our journey began. The train stopped at every station but I slept until daylight arrived. Soon after daylight, at a station, Indian waiters walked along the train. A cup of tea and a slice of buttered toast for – I can't remember how much – just a few annas, but it was a pleasant start to the day. This was not included in our allocated food money. This morning tea and toast was usually offered on Indian trains.

We had also discovered early morning tea in the army in India. At Reveille there was always tea available at the cookhouse. You go along and help yourself. For some reason this custom was known as 'gun fire'.

In our carriage there was a middle aged Englishman, presumably working in India. He chatted to us on the way. There was a washbasin and toilet attached to the carriage and we were able to wash and shave.

We had our breakfast stop, were asked if we wanted dinner, stopped for it – a long stop this one. Then came the stop for the evening meal and so we bedded down for the second night. Our Englishman said our breakfast stop the next morning was Delhi where he would be getting off.

Smaller stations were often almost devoid of travellers, but the main stations were full of people – beggars, people selling food and other things. There was the smell of cigarettes the Indians were smoking.

So far we had been travelling more or less north. From now on it would be north westerly, heading for the Punjab. Somewhere along this stretch we were stopped at a small station while a train passed outside us without stopping. We were told that this was the Frontier Mail.

The next morning we reached Lahore where my companion left the train. I was, in fact, to meet him again for a short period a year later. Lahore is now in Pakistan. Later that day we were to stop at Rawalpindi.

The next day the train was passing through mountainous country. We crossed the River Indus, deep in a gorge, by a spectacular bridge, and, after a couple of hours, reached the end of my journey at Peshawar. Very hot here and sunny. The sun reflecting off white buildings was blinding.

Peshawar is, or was, very much frontier country. The road from here goes to Khyber, the only real way to pass from India into Afghanistan.

The rail transit officer arranged a lift for me to the hospital passing bullock carts and camels on the road, and so to the Military Hospital in the military area some two miles or so from the station.

They were not expecting me, but said I should spend the night and they would give me a rail warrant and travel directions and leave the next day.

PESHAWAR TO BANNU

Razmak is some distance south of Khyber on the frontier. I had to take a train back in the direction of Rawalpindi, crossing the Indus again, to a station called (I think) Cambellpur. Here I caught another train for an overnight journey to Mari Indus to catch a train to Bannu, the railway head for Razmak. I have not mentioned meal stops recently, but they came up automatically.

THE HEAT STROKE EXPRESS

I had now met up with two soldiers from the signals, also heading for Razmak. They had been before and knew the drill. The line to Bannu is a single track, narrow gauge with passing places. It is fairly flat desert, very hot and slow and takes about six hours. It was known as 'The Heat Stroke Express.'

At Mari Indus you collect a small metal bath with a big block of ice in it, from the Rail transport Officer. You also collect a large water container made of leather and canvas. This, placed on the ice, gives cold drinking water for the journey. From Bannu to Razmak by road convoy was over a road picketed and patrolled.

So we took the 'express'. True enough, it was hot and the track was slow. At the dinner stop there was a section of double track where trains could pass. Here there was a group of local people, obviously seeing off a group of friends. They all carried rifles. When the train came, going back the way we had come, those left behind fired their rifles in the air. I wondered what I had been let in for.

So we carried on into Bannu, handed in our bath and our water bottles, and were told that we were lucky, the Razmak road was open the next day. We had charpoy beds to sleep on, under mosquito nets, of course. I had been told that Razmak was too high an altitude for mosquitoes so mosquito nets would not be needed there.

INDIAN LANGUAGES

I was now very much in Pathan country. The men were tall, pale featured and sometimes with hair dyed red. They often carried rifles. The women were not seen. They were in the villages. The language spoken was Pushto, said to be very difficult to learn. All Indians spoke their local language and there were many of them. They quite often spoke Urdu or Hindi as well. The official language of the Raj (British India) was Urdu. Hindi and Urdu as spoken, sounded identical but their written scripts were completely different. Many Indians spoke some English, particularly if they lived in a garrison area. Educated and business Indians spoke fluent English.

IN THE CONVOY TO RAZMAK

The next morning we joined the convoy for Razmak – about twenty lorries with Indian drivers. They were very experienced and used to making this trip.

"Those with rifles in the last truck," we were told, "The rest spread out where you like."

There was occasional sniping at the convoys in which case the last vehicle was better placed to reply. We set off, the road climbing all the time, on a hard but rough road, with rocky hills all round. Occasionally we passed groups of soldiers visible from the road. We made a short stop at a fort half way. This was full of Indian troops and English officers. Beyond this the climb, if anything, got steeper, including a triple zigzag up the side of one hill. Those who had been that way before pointed out the wreck of a truck that had sometime gone over the edge.

HOSPITAL AT RAZMAK

Finally the land levelled out and we passed into Razmak and I found my way into the hospital: mainly a single storey building painted white. Two wards, about ten beds in each with two small side wards. On the first floor was just a small officers' ward. This was the British side. The Indian side was rather bigger. There was a separate operating theatre suite and about twenty British staff.

We slept on metal beds. Accommodation was reasonable. Food, however, was on the short side. There were eggs, tinned meat, chicken, lamb – local produce, real mutton – very tough, needed mincing and boiling. Luckily there was a nearby café, you might call it, where a fried egg and bread sandwich could be purchased – and often was.

RAZMAK TOWN

Razmak was surrounded by a wall that was manned and guarded, especially at night. It was full of military personnel. The 2nd Battalion, the Green Howards, were the British troops on the frontier, and a couple of companies were in Razmak. There were also Ghurkhas present and another Indian battalion. There was also a field ambulance, most of its personnel working in the hospital. There were also men from Signals, etc.

There was a small cinema with a performance every evening, an open-air roller skating rink, (skates available) and several football pitches. A lot of football was played. There was no bazaar in the town although there was a little shop in the hospital. I wanted a pair of football boots and they arrived the next time the road was open.

WORK EXPERIENCE IN THE HOSPITAL LABORATORY

The time here was very useful to us. I had never seen a malaria parasite, nor had I seen dysentery amoeba. They were going to be very common sights for me over the next few years, and here I learned to recognise them. I spent much of my time working in the District laboratory here. The work on bacteria was similar to that I had been doing in England, so, no problem. However, in England, broth and jelly on which we grew bacteria were supplied ready–made. Here they had to be made from scratch. I had experienced doing this during my training but here I had to do it in practice and it was good experience for me.

The climate here was quite nice: like an English summer and there were English type flowers growing in beds by the skating area.

GUN VIOLENCE

When I arrived there were, in the hospital, two men with gunshot wounds, one British and one Indian. The locals were not always friendly and there was certainly the possibility of sniping from outside. At the sound of a gunshot people would try to see where it came from. At night, on a couple of occasions, I was woken by the sound of a machine gun clattering away, and there were parachute flames floating beyond the walls. Some Pathans had been tormenting the guards. I remember playing the Ghurkhas at football. They had a nice grassy pitch outside the walls. The teams met at a gate and, before we were allowed out, about ten Ghurkhas with rifles and a Bren gun went out and settled beyond the touchline. Then we went out with the referee, played the match without problem, and after the match we went back into the camp and our escort came in after us. I can't remember who won but that doesn't matter.

I can't remember whether we spent six or nine weeks in Razmak. It was an experience that very few people had, but I enjoyed it. It was now September, and about time for an extra blanket to be issued for the coming winter, when I was posted away.

JOURNEY TO SECUNDERABAD BY TRAIN

I was posted to 134 Indian Base General Hospital for British Troops (1341BGH, BT), which was at Secunderabad. Secunderabad is on the Decca Plateau in Central India, in Hyderabad State, close to Hyderabad city. So I was off travelling on my own, although at the start there were some Green Howards going off on a few days' leave. There was the road convoy. I waved to friends I had made in the Field Ambulance as we passed them. A night in Bannu, sleeping under a mosquito net again, and then 'the heat-stroke express'. I had a train ticket, of course, but no instructions on track route. I knew I had to get to Delhi and then travel south from there so I took a train to Rawalpindi and from there, through Lahore to Delhi.

From Lahore, in my second-class coach, I found a first class coach next door with a sergeant from the Burma Rifles the sole occupant. He had a first class ticket and he asked me to travel on with him. We both had to change trains at Delhi. I forget where he was going. He said that the Wavell canteen, next to the station, served better food than the station canteen and so we ate there.

I then went to find the train to Secunderabad. I found an Indian Subedhar also looking for the same train. Subedhar is high-ranking Viceroy's Commission, equal to sergeant major or warrant officer. He travelled second class and organised two reserved seats for us. An overnight journey took us to Secunderabad.

SECUNDERABAD ENVIRONS

Secunderabad bordered on Hyderabad city. Hyderabad State was governed by a Hizam, and issued its own currency, although British Indian money was used and was of more value than the Hizam's. About five miles from Secunderabad was a small village called Trimulgherry. This had been a garrison area since the 1800s. Here there had been a fort, extensive barracks, a garrison church and a Military Detention Barracks and Prison, (a 'glass-house'). There was also a small, functioning Indian Military Hospital. There was a bazaar – that is a shopping area, various Indian shops and a cinema. In the area there was also an Indian Armoured Corps Training Centre.

A couple of miles beyond Trimulgherry was another village, Bolarum. Around here there were a number of tented barrack areas, which held, at different times, various British regiments in training or exercising. Here was a small bazaar, a recently built cinema and a wooden building used as a church. Secunderabad itself contained three cinemas and a fair range of shops serving a fairly large number of English or Anglo-Indian civilians. This area had been chosen to be the Base Hospital Area for the Burma Campaign.

THE BASE HOSPITALS: 127, 128, 133, 134

The old brick and stone barrack rooms were in good condition and made fairly good wards. In addition there were some additional new buildings to make extra wards, operating theatres, x-ray units, specialist officers etc. and barrack rooms for the staff. There were to be four Base Hospitals numbered 127,128, 133 and 134.

127 was based in Trimulgherry Fort and not yet working. 128 was partly open, dealing with local British sickness and accidents. 133 was the hospital for Indian troops. It had been the local hospital, now scheduled to be Base Hospital. It was already operational treating local sick and accidents. Secunderabad was to have a convalescent unit.

MY HOSPITAL: BASE 134

To get to my hospital the Rail Transport Officer, at the station, had to ring 133 to collect me and take me to 134. 134, not yet working, had no ambulances. I arrived, found a spare place in a barrack room and deposited my kit. We had metal beds.

There were three plain, functional barrack rooms, each thirty beds, a cookhouse-cum-mess room and a small canteen and shop, with Indians running it. Each barrack room had two bearers - civilian Indian servants. They made our beds, polished our boots and kept the barrack room tidy. This cost one rupee each per week. There was a separate wash block with hand basins and showers.

Washing collected every morning, returned in the evening, no charge. There was a civilian barber. He would come round at, or just before, reveille, and shave you in bed using a cut-throat razor. This would be one rupee per week. He also cut hair and was supplied with a small room for this purpose. Food was reasonable and the canteen sold fried eggs in a buttered roll or in a sandwich. This was the so-called 'egg banjo'. There was also a tea seller (chai wallah) selling tea virtually all day. He had a metal teapot, of sorts, with a tray of smouldering charcoal underneath, keeping the tea hot and stewing it. There was a fruit wallah there at dinnertime, selling oranges and bananas and, sometimes, mangoes.

I found here several men I had travelled from England with. They had been posted here from Deolali and had been involved moving equipment into place.

We were not operational yet, but probably had the staff to do so. The operating theatre, x-ray and laboratory equipment had not all arrived as yet. There was one other laboratory assistant already there and a third arrived a couple of weeks later. I knew him. I had worked with him at Chartham.

TROPICAL DISEASE WORK AT THE DISTRICT HOSPITAL

Near to Trimulgherry Fort was a District laboratory. Each of the four hospitals had its own laboratory, with the District laboratory as back up and to supply medicine etc. There were identical District laboratories in the larger garrison areas in the country. These had done work for the local Military Hospital and also, often for the local Indian civilian hospital.

Number 134 Indian Base Hospital for British Troops, late June 1944. Pte J A Richardson is in the centre of the line of five (with glasses), Clive Newton is seated front left, Tom Taylor front right with dog.

The pathologist, and other doctors in their laboratories, although initially RAMC, became transferred to the IMS - Indian Medical Service. We laboratory assistants were sent to work at the District Laboratory. Very interesting, and we learned a lot more about tropical diseases which we might meet. We hired bicycles in the bazaar, so that we could cycle the three miles to the District Laboratory. In fact many of us hired bikes to travel into Trimulgherry or even to Secunderabad. Bicycle hire was two rupee per month.

OCTOBER 1943: MARKING TIME UNTIL 134 OPENED
This was in October 1943. I think we had enough staff. Doctors had arrived, including some young, female, British ones, and British Nursing Sisters also but still no work for us. The hospital staff now numbered some 100 – 110, excluding doctors and nursing sisters. There was also a number of Indians who were Sweepers (general cleaners), Water Carriers (brought washing water etc.) to bed patients, and Ward Boys who carried bed linen and helped making beds and general fetching and carrying.

On Sunday morning many of us had to attend church parade. Usually we were marched down to the garrison church at Trimulgherry. Looking back, I wish I had paid more attention to church, or particularly to the memorials in the church. It had been there since the 1800s and there were memorials by many regiments, to the number of men who had died while stationed in that area. These deaths were mainly from tropical diseases. However, there was one to someone who had been killed by a tiger.

There were three Base Hospitals in the area, but only one Indian. This balance was wrong. In an Indian Division, Indians outnumber British by almost three to one.

HELPING AT THE INDIAN HOSPITAL
Early in the New Year (1944), Indian patients began arriving in the area and the Indian hospital soon became very busy. As a result, we were asked, (I suppose 'ordered' is a better word) to give assistance. We sent a number of nursing orderlies to work both day and night, on shifts there, using ambulances to run a bus service. I was also sent to help out in their laboratory. This was quite a busy time. The work was mainly microscopic, malaria, dysentery, intestinal worms, an occasional T.B., and, even very occasionally, leprosy. At that time leprosy was incurable. It is not so, now. I hasten to say that leprosy is nowhere as contagious as most people think. There is no danger in touching a leper. This work was interesting. I was working with Indian doctors and Indian orderlies. By this time I had passed the Army Elementary Urdu exam. Although I was never anywhere near fluent, I could make myself understood, and if they spoke to me fairly slowly, I could understand what they were saying to me.

HOSPITAL BASE 134 OPENS WITH 1500 BEDS
By the end of May it was obvious that we should be opening our hospital. We had a dummy run to see how we would manage accepting patients.

There was a rail siding about two miles from the hospital and the hospital trains would arrive there and, with a fleet of ambulances, we would unload patients into the ambulances and, on arriving at hospital, they would be sorted out and transported to the appropriate ward. We thought this went off well.

During the next few months there were changes affecting our uniform. So far we had been wearing khaki drill shorts during the day, trousers after dark. Also, during the day we had to wear topees. First topees were withdrawn, and we went back to wearing our English uniform side caps. Then the wearing of shorts stopped and the khaki drill battle dress was issued. Then the colour changed to green, being a better camouflage colour for jungle conditions, and soon everything was green – socks, towels, underwear –everything. We now had green berets, while in the Burma area, bush hats were worn.

At the beginning of June (D-Day time) we accepted our first train. Trains arrived from two areas. They came from Calcutta and also from Madras. Those from Madras had arrived at Madras by boat. The journey from battlefield to Base Hospital could not take less than four days so none of them were fresh. All had passed through Casualty Clearing Stations and Field Hospitals, and so all had had at least some days of treatment.

So, I can't remember exactly when, but it was just before D-Day, 1944, we stopped working at the Indian hospital and started filling our wards. The hospital had 1500 beds and within two or three weeks it was full.

SHORT STAFFED IN THE LABORATORY

We did not have many battle casualties; ours were mainly diseases. Because of the climate and the jungle conditions, disease put more people in hospital than gunfire, but they did not, in general, take so long to recover. So we had those with malaria, amoebic dysentery, intestinal worms and many who were recovering from fever. At this stage it was not certain which fever. It was thought to be Scrub Typhus and we were usually able to show this to be the case because, in time, their blood showed the development of antibodies to their typhus. I do not remember a single case of typhoid, and certainly none of cholera.

When our hospital started working I had three laboratory assistants. Within two weeks two of them were posted elsewhere, leaving me with a very busy hospital. There was the hospital pathologist and myself. One of our young lady doctors came to work with us. We found a nursing orderly to help prepare samples for us, and we did train him to do blood counts, and then we had a young sweeper boy to do the cleaning and other dirty work. This was the busiest period of my Army life. We worked a six-and-a–half-day week, with an occasional night call out. Sometimes patients remained in hospital for quite long periods. Amoebic dysentery treatment was quite prolonged and if it had not cleared, or they had developed resistant cysts, it might need repeating. Malaria might well return after treatment and then start again. Intestinal worms was not as present in British troops as in Indian troops, but some would have worms and not know it, and we would find it in our routine work. The nasty worm was hookworm, which is very small, has a strong infection cycle and penetrates the feet when walking in wet areas. It finishes up in the gut, just beyond the stomach, where it sucks blood and can cause a nasty anemia. We never found these worms, but the patients are passing their eggs and we find them microscopically. Because of all this, patients often complained that they came into hospital with one thing and caught two others. The truth was that they were incubating them.

We were very busy for four or five months, but as the XIV Army was advancing, fewer sick and wounded were getting back to the Base Hospital area, and so work became less and I was able to have a half day on Saturday and Sunday.

A VISIT FROM ENSA

While this was going on we did have an occasional visit by an ENSA (Entertainments National Service Association) Party – a group of entertainers of various sorts to entertain the Forces. Some were better than others; some contained well-known artists. I never saw Vera Lynn. I remember, particularly, a performance by a Military band – the Band of the Duke of Aosta's regiment – Italian Prisoners-of-War, captured by Gavel's Army in the Western Desert in about 1941. They were captured in entirety – conductor, players, instruments, music: the lot. They toured India as POWs in drab prisoners' uniforms, giving concerts, and they were very good. I was to see them a year or so later. By now, Italy had surrendered and they were no longer prisoners but dressed in uniforms with more gold braid and red tabs than a British General.

I think that the last Hospital Train that we received was on Christmas Eve 1944. The work was easing off very much, by now, and then we had another Lab. Assistant posted to join us. This meant that I could have an occasional day off on a Sunday.

EARLY 1945: WHEN WILL THE WAR END?
By this time, early 1945, it seemed that the War in Europe was heading towards its end, not so the South-East Asian and Pacific War.

There was interest in three subjects: When would the war end? When would we go home? When would we be demobilized?

It was intended that when the war ended, demobilization would take place in an ordered manner. There was a formula, including date of enlistment and age at the time. Two men enlisted on the same day - the older would go first. This gave a number called 'Age and Service Number'.

There was also an Overseas Service Number. This was years and days overseas counted from a particular date in early 1944. This would determine when you would be repatriated once the war was finished. While the war was in progress, six years' service overseas was needed before repatriation. From VE Day this was reduced to five years, and slowly reduced from this.

SPORTS AND LEISURE AT SECUNDERABAD
I have said nothing about sport possibilities at Secunderabad. We had a tennis court, a hockey pitch and a football pitch. A lot of hockey and football were played. Three barrack rooms played each other at hockey. The Sergeants' Mess and the Officers' Mess were also involved. The Officers' team included some lady doctors and Nursing Sisters. No one was mad enough to hit the Colonel's ankles. Football was played against local units and there were occasional

games between British players and Indians. The Indians often played barefoot.

We also had a Hospital Concert Party, which gave an occasional performance to both staff and patients. It included Nursing Sisters as well as Orderlies. We had a small orchestra: a trumpet, a clarinet, a violin and quite a good pianist. We had to hire the piano. This was delivered to the hospital on foot - two rows of four men, with the piano on its back, lifted it and rested it on the four heads and they walked, carrying it for something like five miles.

We had a couple of singers and a very good magician. I think we enjoyed the performance; at least we applauded.

POSTING TO FIELD LABORATORY
Some time in mid-1944, I had made a request to be posted to a Field Laboratory. General Hospitals (Field Hospitals), formed in England, had a full laboratory staff in their complement and came out fully equipped. These usually came out as part of a British Division. Hospitals formed in India did not have laboratory staff, as personnel and equipment were in short supply. Instead individual Field Laboratories were formed consisting of one or two pathologist / doctors, one British assistant and five or six Indians including a clerk. A Field Laboratory could move and set up much quicker than a General Hospital. It could work from tents if necessary. It could do work for two hospitals or Casualty Clearing Stations. It had no cooking facilities and so, needed support of this nature.

JOURNEY TO CHITTAGONG
Early in April I received instructions to travel to Chittagong for onward transmission. I found out later that my destination was 50 Indian Field Laboratory, wherever it might be.

Chittagong is in what is now Bangladesh – 50 or so miles from the border with Burma. First there was a train journey to Calcutta. This lasted two days, involved two trains. I found a traveller from one of the other hospitals, and two RAF men travelling in the same direction. At Calcutta I spent a day and a half in the transit camp.

I had been in India for eighteen months and thought I was used to the climate. Razmak was similar to an English summer. Secunderabad was hot. It had a monsoon season but a rather mild and short one. It was bearable. Calcutta was not as hot as Secunderabad but it was on the coast and the atmosphere was very humid. It also had a long, heavy monsoon. I had to endure this for the rest of my stay overseas.

From Calcutta I was sent to the Reinforcement Camp at Chittagong. There is no direct road across south Bengal. The delta stream of the Ganges and Brahmaputra Rivers get in the way. From Calcutta I took a train at midnight, travelling roughly northwards.

To reach the train you had to tread carefully over the beggars sleeping on the ground. The train was narrow gauge, and the carriages were rather primitive, and it was full of XIVth Army men travelling back to Burma. Most of them had made the journey before. The XIVth Army was the army in the Burma campaign. There seemed to be a lot of an RAF regiment on the train. As it got light the next morning the train was slowly making its way alongside the Brahmaputra River. There was a mess room there where a very good breakfast was served, and then we boarded a ferryboat.

We spent about six hours slowly sailing along the Brahmaputra River. The war was still on, of course, and we had four Bren gunners posted on the top deck in case of Japanese planes. It did not matter that the nearest Japanese were about 500 miles away. The ferry finally deposited us at, I think, Laksam.

A further overnight train took us to Chittagong where a truck took me, and several others, to the Reinforcement Camp about five miles outside.

REINFORCEMENT CAMP: CHITTAGONG

The British section of this camp was a flat area on top of a hill. There were twenty or thirty tents, each comfortably housing four or six men. They had been there some time and some were rather badly worn.

You slept on the ground on a ground sheet, mosquito net suspended from beneath the roof. If it rained, as it often did, sometimes the tent would leak. Then, if you had a second ground sheet or a monsoon cape, you did your best to position it on top of the mosquito net to divert the water.

This was mosquito country so you were fed one anti-malarial a day, plus a vitamin tablet. I had spent over a year in central India, where it was very hot but the atmosphere, on the whole, rather dry. Here it was not quite so hot, but very humid and this was very unpleasant. During the day it was customary to go shirtless, once your skin had become accustomed to the sun. This took me three very careful weeks. Because of this, below the waist we were white, above the waist brown, with some, near black.

After dark you wore a shirt. In less than an hour it was wet with sweat. Next morning it was hung up to dry and worn again the next evening, and so on until you managed to wash it. If you drank a cup of tea it would immediately sweat out. If you were sitting down, on getting up you would leave behind a wet patch. Men had to fight like this.

Water was at the bottom of the hill – from a hand pump. There were no washbasins or showers.

Dehydrated potato and other things came in tins of two-gallon size. With the top cut off and a short length of wood nailed across the open top, you had a handy water container. Problem: How do you wash down using a two-gallon can of water from the pump? Well, it can be done. You do need a friend to tip the water over you at the end, for a rinse.

Cookhouse also was at the bottom of the hill by the water pump. Food here was very good; as good as any army food I had in India. Special treat on Sundays – tinned spuds.

The dining room had been a basha – a hut made of bamboo, but this had recently blown down in a storm, although it was being rebuilt. At the moment it was a large tent.

There were no plates. We had to use our Mess tins. These were in two pieces. If you have porridge in one and tea in the other, what do you do with a piece of bacon, or a rissole, or a fish cake? There may also be some potato. Probably you would have it on a slice of bread. The same problem arose most meal times, but we survived and were reasonably happy. We had all been some time abroad and were used to hardships. I was in that camp long enough to see some new arrivals direct from England. They had come across India, direct to Chittagong, and it was a culture shock to them.

As a recruit in 1942 I had fired rifle and Bren guns. Here I had revision firing in both, plus revolver, Sten gun, Tommy gun, and also threw live hand grenades. We thought we were going to what could be a fighting area, and needed to be able to defend ourselves if necessary. A red cross was no defence against the Japanese, and some medical corps men had had to rearm to defend themselves. There were some twenty or so other RAMC men in that camp, together with a number from fighting units, some of whom had seen action.

There was a good canteen in the camp, and a cinema, although on the occasion that I sampled the cinema, it showed the reels in a haphazard order. On Saturday and Sunday there was a truck to Chittagong for anybody who wanted to go. Chittagong had a cinema, Chinese restaurants and a bazaar.

VE DAY
While I was here VE occurred, May 8th, 1945.We were given a free meal at the canteen, and also a bottle of beer, free. We were told that there was sufficient beer in the canteen for an extra three bottles each – to be paid for – and there was an additional payday so that we could buy it. Those of us that did not want the addition were happy for their friends to buy it. It was American beer and not particularly pleasant I was told.

DISPATCHED TO A LABORATORY ON THE MOVE
I was then posted to 50th Indian Field Laboratory at a hospital at Akhaura, some six or seven hours rail journey away from Chittagong. I went but it was no longer there, and the hospital was closing down and preparing to move also. Rangoon had been reoccupied on May 1st and reinforcements were going to Burma by sea, via Rangoon.

BACK TO 'FORGOTTEN' CHITTAGONG
I had to return to Chittagong and it seemed that most waiting there were forgotten.

I found out later that while I was in the Reinforcement Camp, the Field Laboratory was in the port area of the town, waiting to go to Rangoon by sea. They had lost their British lab assistant to sickness and had acquired one from a laboratory working in a Chittagong general hospital. The local RAMC control did not appear to know what was happening. Even when 50th Laboratory had sailed, I could easily have replaced the one they had borrowed, so filling the vacancy left in Chittagong. So the Reinforcement Camp knew I was booked for 50th Laboratory but did not know where it was.

The result was that I stayed, and there seemed to be no movement, at all, of anybody from the camp. Chittagong seemed to be a dead area as far as movement was involved.

OPEN AIR FILMS
While I was away, trying to locate my posting, the cinema in the camp had burned down. I then experienced an open-air film show. In the tropics, night falls quickly. By seven o'clock the light has gone and, with no outside lamps, darkness is complete. A mobile cinema consisted of a box type van with projector, electric generator, loudspeakers and a portable screen. The screen is erected in a field a suitable distance from the projector, and the film is shown. The audience sit or squat in the dark to watch the show. Even if it rains they can still see the film. This was quite a common entertainment in this area.

CAMP COMILLA
After some weeks there was a decision to close this camp, and we were taken, by road, to another camp at Comilla. Here we lived and slept in bashas and the beds were bamboo benches: quite comfortable and better than sleeping on the ground in tents. Food was not so good here. We were in addition to the British troops already waiting here. There was also a large quantity of Indian troops in one adjacent camp.

JAPAN SURRENDERS - END OF WAR!

While here we had news of the atom bombs and the surrender of Japan. The sudden end of war was a complete surprise and also a great relief.

At the end of the war in Europe we had thought in terms of another two years for the war against the Japs and we did not look on it as a great prospect.

At this point, the XIV Army, which was by far the largest army of World War II, was split and from it a new XII Army had been formed.

We found out later that the new XIV would be involved in a landing on the coast of Malaya, while the XII was to advance eastward into Siam. We were now XII Army.

ALL RAMC PERSONNEL HEAD TO RANGOON

Now there was movement - all RAMC personnel back to Calcutta and, by sea, to Rangoon. There were some forty or so of us from Chittagong who went by train to the Brahmaputra Ferry, from the ferry to train to Calcutta and on to a boat bound for Rangoon. The sea journey took five days – not very comfortable, but uneventful.

We moored at a floating landing-stage, in the middle of the Rangoon River, and went by landing ship to the shore, and by truck to the Forward Advanced Reinforcement Holding Unit (This is what it was called.) We were each asked where we thought we were going. One night was spent under canvas. The next morning I was taken by road to 58th Indian General Hospital where 50th Indian Field Laboratory was working. The roads in Rangoon were terrible – full of potholes.

50TH INDIAN FIELD LABORATORY: RANGOON

The hospital was in what had been Rangoon Medical School. I found two doctors: one an Indian who had been a GP in England, the other was a Punjabi. He was Indian but was now termed Pakistani. Both were very competent and also very friendly. There was also the British lab assistant they had acquired in Chittagong. He was a Sergeant by now. I was a Corporal. There was an Indian Clerk, a Havildar, equivalent to a

Sergeant in the British Army. There were also four Indian sepoys. The laboratory equipment was first class except there was no gas or electricity. It relied on oil burners and primus stoves for heating. It also had oil-operated refrigerators. The hospital overflowed into what had been a convent on the other side of the road.

At this time British Prisoners of War, released from the Japanese, were still being recovered and, although the hospital was for Indian Troops, there were many British now lying on mattresses in the corridors. But within a couple of days these had gone. Once they were considered fit to travel they were on their way, first to transit camps, then back to England to be demobilized. There were other Indian General Hospitals in Rangoon: one in the Rangoon High Court, one in the university and a British general Hospital in the dock area. British prisoners needing medical treatment were in the British Hospital or the one at the university.

The hospital I was now with had an Indian staff, with the exception of the small number of East Africans. There were two East African Hospital Units – equivalent to a small Field Ambulance. There were two British East African officers, three British Sergeants and, say, seventy or so East African soldiers.

In the general Hospital, as it was, all the doctors were Indian. There was one British officer. He was the unit Quartermaster. The only English soldiers were myself, the other laboratory assistant and the three English Sergeants with the East Africans. We lived in what had been a lodge of the convent, sleeping on camp beds. Food came to us from the Officer's Mess and so our food was a mixture of British type and curry.

DEMOBILIZATION CRITERIA

With the end of the war, demobilization had begun using age and Service numbers. The first to go, within the main, were those who had been called up aged twenty-one or nearby, at the start of the war. These had served around six years in the army and so deserved to go. Also, the maximum period of service overseas was reduced to five years. So before long, anyone who had left England in early 1941 would be due for repatriation.

I was very happy working in this hospital but it did not last for long. We were visited by a full Colonel, the Director of Pathology, XIV Army. He visited all the Rangoon hospitals.

TRANSFER TO 55 IFU FIELD LABORATORY

The hospital in the High Court building (49 I.G.H.) had a Field Laboratory working for it, (55 I.F.U.), which was very short of staff. It only had one doctor pathologist; the other one had been repatriated. It had lost its Sergeant Lab. Assistant somewhere and was overworked. I was posted here as a result.

The hospital was also dealing with Indian patients but it had a number of British RAMC orderlies on its staff, unlike the hospital I was leaving which had none. Also, as well as British Nursing Sisters, it had a number of VAD nurses. This hospital was three storeys high and built around four sides of a square. We were on the top floor, above which rose a short clock tower. Our Indian staff slept in the clock tower. We slept across the road in a building of two floors – quite comfortable. There were generators to supply electricity.

POST MORTEMS

This field laboratory had arrived in Rangoon before 49 I.G.H. and, to give itself some work to do before the hospital arrived, had agreed to do all the post-mortem examinations requested by the Military Police for forensic purposes, and this it continued to do. I thus found myself involved with road accidents, drownings, suicides, two murders etc. during my stay. At that time I had a very good stomach.

CAROLS ON CHRISTMAS EVE

I spent Christmas, 1945 here. The hospital matron, from somewhere, had found some Salvation Army members now in the British Army in Rangoon. They had their instruments and, on Christmas Eve, we had carols in the square inside the High Court building. Meanwhile Rangoon Cathedral had been cleaned up and rededicated, and was crowded for the midnight service; the first service of Peace.

Rangoon was slowly getting back to something like normal. Mains electricity was restored and water was on tap. They wanted us out but, in the meanwhile, would like their High Court and Medical School back.

Sometime fairly early in the New Year, 1946, I can't remember exactly when, all patients in the hospital were transferred to the other two hospitals in Rangoon. With the end of the fighting there was now less work for the hospitals, and 49 I.G.H. was told to pack up ready to move. It was subsequently moved to Meiktila in Central Burma. There was already a Field Laboratory there so we were not needed.

TREATING SEXUALLY TRANSMITTED DISEASES

In Rangoon there was a Beach Medical Unit. It had been supplying Field Ambulance Services to several sea landings that had taken place at a number of islands up the Burmese coast, from Chittagong to Rangoon. It now had nothing to do. It had been formed into a unit to treat Sexual Transmitted Diseases among Indian and African troops. There were West African troops, two Divisions of them, in the XIV Army.

They had been found an Indian Consultant and also, three or four British Army orderlies, trained in dealing with diagnosis and treatment of STDs. 55th Indian Field Laboratory was to go and work for them.

At this time the Burmese had been given back the Medical School where 58 I.G.H. and 50th Field Laboratory had been working. That hospital had already overflowed into what had been Rangoon convent. The hospital moved from the medical School, filling up the Convent accommodation which had also housed a fairly large number of RAF Regiment who had now moved on and this left room for the one time Beach Medical Unit and us. So we moved again.

Work here was interesting but we were not very busy, although my Urdu was useful. The consultant here, an Indian Major, rather unusually, liked western classical music. He had a wind-up gramophone and of an evening would sometimes play his records to us.

After a while, we were visited again by the Director of Pathology who said that he had not yet decided whether the Field Lab. would be left to function or disbanded. At this time Field Laboratories were being absorbed into the hospitals they had been working for.

The Indian doctor/pathologist I had been working for was posted to join a laboratory with the hospital that had just moved from Rangoon to Meiktila. He was replaced by another Indian doctor. So now I had a new boss.

RETURN TO INDIA?

This did not last. A few weeks later it was decided to disband the Field laboratory and send its records back to India. I was asked, would I like to go to India? No I would not.

So the laboratory disappeared. Not being told where to go, I moved to the laboratory in the hospital, now completely in the convent. The British sergeant and the Indian staff were still there. The two officers had gone. The British Indian had been repatriated and the Indian had been demobilized. The laboratory was now controlled by an Anglo – Indian doctor – no problem. I think that, at this time, I should have been posted to Meiktila, as, later, I met an Indian from Meiktila Hospital who told me that I had been expected there.

I was happy where I was and we were busy. This must have been about May 1946. The former Beach Medical Unit, which was next door, was now absorbed into this hospital. So we now had a British staff of five.

HOSPITAL FOOTBALL TEAM

We had a hospital football team, part British, part Indian, and a football pitch, and there were many football pitches nearby. There were two football leagues running: one between units that were completely British and the other between mixed teams. We were playing during the monsoon season. At times, the pitches were half covered with water. The football might not have been good, but we enjoyed it.

CULTURAL VARIETY

Initially the Mobile Film Unit came round fairly regularly. Then the Rangoon cinema was refurbished and showed films regularly. Rangoon Theatre was also repaired and refurbished and there were regular entertainments. We had a ballet company, music by two pianos. We had plays – John Gielgud came, Tommy Trinder – if you know who he was – also, a very good concert pianist who played non-stop for over an hour. There was even Bob Hope. I did not see him. I think he gave just one performance during the day and I was working. We again saw the Italian Military Band.

By this time the Overseas Service limit was down to three-and-a-half years. I had done three so my time was coming.

JAPANESE POWs HAD CHOLERA

During this period we had patients with cholera in the hospital. They were Japanese Prisoners of War. We had to refer to them as Japanese Surrendered Personnel (PC as early as that). They were being concentrated at Rangoon before being shipped home. They were on their way by boat from Moulmein in southern Burma to Rangoon when the outbreak began. We had 25 to 30 of them in a ward that led out from the laboratory so we had a guard of armed Ghurkhas who grinned at us but terrified the Japanese. Three had died on the ship but all those who entered the hospital survived. This is the only time that I encountered cholera.

Then in early July I was posted to Medan in Sumatra. This was stupid; I had only months left to serve before I would go home. At first I was told I must go then they thought again and said no. At that moment Overseas Service was reduced to three years and I had been away just over three years.

WAITING FOR THE BOAT HOME

I moved into the Transit Camp third week in July, was issued with British Battle Dress, filled in the required forms and waited for the boat. There must have been three or four hundred army personnel to sail, from a variety of different units – around forty from RAMC, some returning to be demobilized, others who had completed their three years or so, overseas.

ON BOARD THE LINER 'CARTHAGE'

The troopship arrived and was anchored in the river. It was a P&O liner, 'Carthage', converted for troops and painted smartly in black and white, not the drab grey of those we had come out in. It brought reinforcements or replacements for those who were leaving, plus a few returning from home leave.

I had packed a kit bag full, to go in the hold, and a smaller sea kitbag to carry on board. We were taken by trucks to the harbour there, by a landing barge to the ship.

Here we did not have mess decks. There was a large dining room with fixed tables, and we queued to collect our food. Food was reasonable. Sleeping accommodation was separate. We had metal-framed mesh bunks (almost like shelves), in tiers of four, hooked up during the day, let down at night. We were crowded but they were comfortable. We were joined on the boat by an equally large number of RAF, plus some marines and sailors.

Once on board, we sailed without delay. On shore we could see men waving, and waving flags and anything else they could find, some from roofs and others from windows. There was an RAF Dakota flying around, men on board it also waving and also a smaller aircraft circling quite close. So we said goodbye to Rangoon and Burma.

The ship's hospital was soon seeking medical orderlies and a laboratory assistant and so I found myself a job for the voyage. I was needed. I did confirm, microscopically, two cases of malaria, very likely relapses, and a number of cases of amoebic dysentery - fifteen or so. I thought this was a bit excessive but a doctor from the RAF camp said it was in line with the number of cases he had been finding in their transit camp.

The journey passed off incident-free. A short stop of only one day, at Colombo, Ceylon, then non-stop.

SUEZ CANAL

It was interesting to pass through the Suez Canal. To those of us who came round The Cape this was a new experience. Britain still garrisoned the canal area and so we were to see British soldiers as we passed through. A few days and we were to pass Gibraltar and enter the Atlantic.

We had been expecting to dock at Southampton but there was a dock strike, so now we were told Tilbury. It would mean another half day or so at sea. Then we were told, late one evening, we should see the lights of England and some did stay up to see them.

WHITE CLIFFS OF DOVER

Next morning we awoke to see the white cliffs. We passed Dover and saw the anti-aircraft fort built off Deal in the early days of the war, and then passed into the Mouth of the Thames and saw anti-aircraft platforms there.

At that time there were steamer trips from Tower Pier in London, to Southend and then to Herne Bay or Margate and we soon heard that one of them was approaching. We all moved over to the side to shout and wave to them and they did the same to us. This was our first welcome home.

DOCKING AT TILBURY

Then, in the afternoon, we docked at Tilbury with German Prisoners of War using trucks to unload our kitbags.

The ship contained many groups; some quite small, going to different parts of the country. Issuing of group railway tickets and sorting out timetables was a problem.

THE 3.30AM TRAIN TO FLEET

The first groups caught a train at about ten o'clock in the evening. Our train was to go at three-thirty a.m. One of the groups was called to collect the party ticket for about twenty of us, with Fleet, Hampshire being the destination that was for the RAMC depot at Crookham.

We collected our kitbags from the Passenger Hall and boarded the train, which took us around the east and north of London to Saint Pancras, then underground to Waterloo, arriving there during the morning rush hour. We were fairly conspicuous, all wearing bush hats and carrying kitbags. Several former XIV army men, on their way to work, spoke to us. Then to Fleet. Now we had some RAMC doctors with us. A truck took us to Crookham and the depot.

We had hoped to be sent home that day but because they had to supply each of us with tickets, Ration books, Leave Passes and give us some pay, this would take time. So we spent the night in barrack rooms and were sent off next morning. Most of us phoned or telegrammed family to say what time to expect us.

MY FAMILY MET ME AT WATERLOO

We ordered enough taxis to take us to Aldershot station, Aldershot having better train service than Fleet. My family met me at Waterloo. This was August 23rd 1946. My previous leave had finished May 8th 1943.

Twenty-eight days later we were back in Crookham during which time a group of us went into Fleet and had a fish and chip supper before we were split up and posted away.

I had hoped that I might be posted to a hospital in Germany since I still had some time left before my Age & Service Number would be reached for my demobilization. Instead I was posted to the Royal Army Medical College in London, to act as instructor for the trainee lab. assistants on the course there.

MILITARY HOSPITAL AT MILLBANK

So I went to Millbank, just off the river, a short distance beyond Westminster. Here was the home of the staff of the Military Hospital at Millbank. It suited me because at that time I lived in Essex and had many relations living in east London.

At the college there were two other instructors, a young lab. assistant on the staff as well. They were Regular soldiers with quite a few years of service, and there were eight students on the course. The college

also ran training courses on bacteriology for Army doctors. These were instructed by two Regular officers, one a Colonel, the second a Major who I had worked with in the District Laboratory at Secunderabad back in 1943/44.

The college had a collection of various bacteria and while I was there I also had the job of looking after this collection, regularly transferring them to fresh media so that it did not die out.

While here I was able to go home on Saturday afternoons and catch a train at six o'clock on Monday morning to get back in time for breakfast at eight. I also got home for Christmas and had a week's leave.

SEVERE WINTER 1946/47

This winter of 1946/47 was extremely bitter and, following three years in the tropics, was quite a shock.

We were half a dozen Sergeants sleeping in a barrack room, for most of us, following tropical service. If anyone went on leave we shared his blankets until he returned.

DEMOBILIZATION LEAVE

My age and service group was due for demobilization in February 1947. On demobilization everyone was entitled to a period of demob. leave. During this time you received your army pay and allowances, and, at the end, you were transferred to what was known as Z Reserve, to be recalled only in severe emergencies. A few were called back during the Korean War.

Demobilization leave was, I think, eight weeks – at least judging from the length of leave I had. There was also additional leave at the rate of one day for every month spent overseas. I had thirty-nine months abroad and thirty-nine days extra.

DEMOBILIZATION

I was demobilized on February 28th 1947. A Demob. Booklet had to be completed, and details of your service entered. It included an Army Reference and pieces that were removed as you went through the

Demob. Centre, and other pieces that were stamped as you passed through.

Then you collected your civilian clothes: a shirt, a suit – all with choices, a pair of shoes (I think), and a hat or cap. This was neatly packed for you in a cardboard box with fitted lid and carrying handle. You were recognizable as just demobbed on your way from the Demob. Centre. You kept one battle dress, one pair of boots, all underwear, etc. You could also keep your greatcoat but this, I think, cost you eight pounds.

I went home entitled to thirteen weeks leave. I spent four weeks at home. It was bitterly cold; it snowed and snow lay thick on the ground.

After four weeks I returned to work in the laboratory of the factory where I had been working when called up.

My demob. leave ended June 4th, 1947. I had spent four years and eleven months in the army.

'I AM NOT PROUD OF MY ARMY SERVICE'
I am not proud of my army service. I had an easy time. I was in little, if any, danger. There was a little sniping on the North West Frontier, but these were the only shots I heard fired in anger during my time in the army.

The army decided the work that I was to do, moving me from Signals to Medical Corps. This, I suppose, was to them, a reasonable move in view of my civilian occupation and I was only one of several moved at that time. Someone had to do this work. I agree it was reasonably interesting, and I think I did reasonably well, but I wanted to play a more active part.

As a result of where I was and at what time, I am entitled to wear four medals, which I don't think I earned, although I do polish them up and wear them on Remembrance Day and also for funerals of local Burma Star holders.

Margaret Mason, nee Fiddler

Norma Hagon

WHERE WAS I ON VE DAY?
In Manchester suburbs – Winton near Eccles. Woken up by neighbours shouting for us to get up quick – The War's Over!! All the street gathered and we had a party, bonfire and any food everyone could muster. Those men who were around (on leave) chopped trees down to make the fire a really good spectacle. I remember asking my mother the next day "What will they put in the newspapers from now on!"

Frances Cleaver, nee Rush

WORKING IN MUNITIONS AND LAND ARMY
I was 14 when war broke out. I had just left school. I worked at a munition factory in Thame. Three years after this, I went in the Land Army and drove vehicles to the fields. The tractors pulled the combine harvesters. I lived in a hostel in Buckingham Street, Aylesbury, next door to where the fish and chip shop is. The hostel was just for girls. I also worked in Bucks War Aid offices in Turnfurlong where all the machinery was kept.

STARTING WORK AT GROVE HOSPITAL
1939 was my last year at school. I left school when I was 14. I went to work in the kitchens at Grove Hospital in Leighton Buzzard. The hospital had patients with scarlet fever and diphtheria. I worked there for two years.

MY NEXT JOBS
I then worked for Wing Commander Biggs and his wife in Church Cottage next to Mentmore Church. I cleaned and looked after the children. It was very hard work. I left after one year and went to work at Irvings Farm down Long Marston Road.

WORKING AT GOSSARDS
Then I went into war work at Gossards in Leighton Buzzard. They made parachutes, rubber dinghies and barrage balloons. The only bras and corsets made were for the forces.

Jack H. Smith

ROS WORRELL'S FATHER

WHERE WAS I ON VE DAY 1945?

I thought a bit, couldn't remember, then I did, but like all good stories there's a start and a finish, so here goes. What's this to do with VE Day? When you pass 92 you live in the past, so here we go. It's September 1939. I had a wonderful job, not in my birthplace, which was Burnley in Lancashire, but in south Devon, Dartington Hall. It was the English base for The Russian Ballet, comprising all the world's best ballet dancers. I was pally with the leading male, a friend, a German, Rudolf Pesse.

THOUGHT WAR WOULD BE OVER BY CHRISTMAS!

However, war was declared, and being a patriotic idiot I left Devon, returning to Burnley and volunteered for the army, thinking it would be over by Xmas 1939. Yes we were very gullible in those days.

CANAL TO DUNKIRK

Now after a winter in France extending the Maginot Line, six of us were sent to Lille, three high ranking officers informed us we were to take a barge to Dunkirk, via the canal. We were in the first (motor engine) and towed the second barge. Should we have any trouble and have to leave, the boats were to be sunk. The canal was our home for three days.

SWIMMING WITH A SWASTIKA!

After an eventful journey we arrived in Dunkirk, civilians of all ages were coming from Holland and Belgium etc, with youngsters not knowing where to go or where to stay. A very new aspect on war. One episode I well remember, all the farms were deserted along the waterfront. Planes came over, I was having a swim, no one about when I looked up at a plane not yards above me, the pilot waved down, I waved back and then I saw the swastika!! However I got a lift on a boat back to England. After a few days, Dunkirk was all fires with the bombs and shells falling.

THOUGHTS ON THE WAR

Although I was in Africa, Malta, Sicily and Scotland, later France, Brussels, Holland, I never forgot the Dutch and Belgian civilians, no home, no country, families lost. I got back to England O.K. Train took us all to Cornwall. The barracks did us proud. I got into a clean uniform and got a week-end pass to Dartington Hall, always a beautiful place. Then down to Southend to await the Germans. Fortunately for us they didn't cross the channel.

Well having been around a bit I broke my ankle while in Germany and was moved back to a Canadian Military Hospital in Westphalia. Then on to an army convalescent hospital at Blankenberg in Belgium. We all heard that Blighty was the next stop, alas German prisoners were coming back so we had to stay.

Now to where I was on VE Day? I have still got a snap of myself with a Burnley lad on the beach at Blankenberg, Belgium, looking across the waters at Dunkirk, still smoke coming from the place 5 years after we had left it.

Pamela Buckley Daniels

(Interviewed by granddaughter Laura Steed for a Cheddington School Project). Pamela is Gail Steed's mother.

SELBY

I was 12 years old when the Second World War started and was living in Selby, Yorkshire. I can't remember a lot of change to the food that we ate but I think my mother must have been very clever with the rations. The food that was hard to get was meat, butter, sugar, oranges and bananas and anything that came from abroad.

During the blackouts we were not to show any light at all and we had to have blackout curtains made to keep the light in. If we showed a chink of light the Air Raid Warden would come and tell us to close the curtains in a better way.

If there was an air raid the sort of safe place we would go to would usually be an air raid shelter, or, if you hadn't got a shelter a safe place would be under the stairs or under a table.

I wasn't an evacuee but we had a little evacuee came to live with us who came from Hull and he was a little boy about 7 or 8. He was very homesick and didn't stay with us for very long - he had to go home in the end. After that we had an army officer stay with us. There were a lot of army billeted in Selby and this very nice officer lived with us but I don't remember that we fed him so I presume there was an army mess somewhere where he had his food.

YORK

Later on, we didn't stay in Selby for all the war, we moved to York as my father had a job in a bank but that was very bad as they were bombing so we moved onto the Yorkshire Moors to Goathland where we were safe and away from the bombing.

GERRARDS CROSS

I then went away to a school down in the south of England about 10 miles from London called Maltman's Green at Gerrards Cross. I remember the flying bombs coming over and they were called Doodlebugs - they were like automatic planes that didn't have pilots in them, they were really bombs and made a very loud noise when they went over. When the engine stopped we knew then that the bomb was going to fall but usually we didn't get that as they were on their way to London. They had to come over us to go to London.

The school had shelters and at one stage when the war was at its height we had to go into the shelters every night and we all had our own bunk.

Peter Sharp

SCHOOL AND APPRENTICESHIP

I was born in 1928. I was 11 when war broke out and at Denbigh School in Luton. I then went to Luton Tech to train to be an engineer. In 1944 I was an apprentice at George Kent Ltd. In 1946 I was making water meters.

SHOULD I BE EVACUATED?

I did have the opportunity to be evacuated to Canada by boat, but two convoy ships of evacuees were sunk, so Mum went off the idea.

CHILDREN HAD FUN PLAYING AT WAR

During the war it was a hell of a lot of fun if you were at school. The army were setting sandbanks and gun placements in Luton and the children were playing at war.

V2 DEATHS IN LUTON

A V2 fell on Kent's factory and killed the Scoutmaster and about 20 others. Dr O'Meara was killed and all his patients. A V2 fell on Biscot Road Luton and demolished Commer Cars. Most of the secretaries were badly injured. A V2 could take a whole street down. They were building V2s in Peenemunde, Germany, and they were also fired from France.

Anonymous Tring

I lived in New Mill, Tring and there was a Victory Parade with torches. My torch was quite heavy and consisted of a thick piece of wood with some kind of material wrapped round the end and dipped in oil or tar (I think.) My arms ached so much that I was frightened of burning the pixie-hood of the girl in front. The march finished in Grove Road, Tring with a fun fair and a girl who lived near us badly broke her ankle on a 'Savey Sally'.

We lived in Icknield Crescent (now called Icknield Green) and we had a marvellous tea on the Green. We had a large tin of pineapple chunks and each child had one cube. One neighbour dressed up as Old Mother Riley and her daughter dressed as Kitty.

In 1946, when I was 18, I had to choose between being a Bevin boy (which meant working down the coal pits) or to join up. I chose to go in the Air Force.

E. A. Wild

VE DAY

I was nine years old and remember being woken up to be told that the war was over. I thought it was another air raid because I was in Islington, London, very near to the City of London which was constantly bombed.

My sister and myself were evacuated to Nelson in Lancashire to escape the Blitz. I cannot remember how long we were there but it seemed forever. We were back in London when the war ended. I can remember sleeping in an Anderson Shelter which was always six inches deep in water. My dad was in the army and a Dispatch Rider. All my mother's family used to sleep in our house. My uncle was a black-cab driver and my aunt was a waitress in the West End. He always used to pick her up after work and one night during an air raid they pulled into Poland Street Garage for safety, but it sustained a direct hit. They never found my aunt but Uncle Jack was still alive under tons of rubble. I used to have a cutting of the Daily Mirror about a Doctor who crawled down to save him and, although he did not, he was awarded the George Medal.

George Mason

THE VILLAGE SCHOOL

I was born at Blenheim Cottages by the crossroads and I went to the village school until I was fourteen. Mr Jeffery was the Headmaster. He had a mirror so that he could see what we were doing in the other part of the classroom. He would summon us with his index finger. There were canings across our hands. I said that I was going to tell my father so he gave me a hiding on my backside! Miss Alderman taught the infants in one room. Miss Nellie Bosworth had Standard 1. They taught us right from wrong. They had prayers every morning and Scripture lessons, then it came to arithmetic and then, perhaps, a book to read and different things. We had woodwork and gardening.

AFTER SCHOOL PLAY

At night we used to play on the Green. There were laurel hedges at the corners – perfect for Hide and Seek. They pulled the fence up to make it a bit bigger. I remember when we was up the station there used to be privet hedges by the cottages. When they used to come from the station we used to get a parcel – tied on a bit of string and hide in the bushes. Then we snatched it away as they came. We used to do a bit of window tapping with a drawing pin and a bit of cotton. And we used to knock on doors and run away!

FATHER'S SHOP

My father left the farm during the 1930s, to start a shop in the village High Street next to the original Chapel, which is now a private house. He bought the premises, from Mr. Howlett, which had a petrol pump and an oil tank in the yard. He filled a smaller tank – about 200 gallons – with oil, put it on the cart along with cleaning stuff – Persil, Vim and a few bits and pieces if they wanted them – a new wick, or globe or something like that, and pulled by a horse. He used to take it round the villages – Ivinghoe, Ivinghoe Aston, Mentmore, Long Marston, Marsworth – different villages on different days – selling oil for heating, lighting and cooking. Then he started the shop a bit

later on. He had a green shed up the yard, which was rented to an American Officer for a while, and another for Persil and that sort of thing. I sometimes used to go into Aylesbury on the train to order petrol or paraffin, before I went to school.

THE WAR BEGINS

I remember the announcement of war on the radio. I was eleven years old.

George Pennell always reckoned the first bombs to fall locally were at Mentmore in 1940. They fell near the spinney. We boys went up to see them and to collect bits of them. The bombs broke the land drainage pipes and then the fields always flooded.

There were crosses made of tree trunks laid in the fields to stop the enemy planes from landing. There were three or four up the side of Mentmore Park to stop them landing in the road.

There was a Royal Observer Corps lookout point on West Hill, which was manned by three brothers – Ern, George and Bill Pennell, amongst others.

We used to stand at the fence where we could see the ack-ack of the anti aircraft guns in London. You could see the shells go up and burst.

I remember the older men used to come to their gates and I would hear them calling out to each other – my dad to Alcock, Alcock to George Ing, George Ing to Mr Keck Wesley and Keck to John Wesley. They used to come to their gates to see who was about.

LEISURE

There were four pubs in the village: The Rosebery, The Old Swan, The Three Horseshoes and The Old Inn, which was on The Green and only a beer one.

The Yanks and the RAF used to attend dances in what is now the Scout Hut. That was our only hall in the village. If you walked up Mentmore Park there were couples everywhere and they used to say there were more bodies made than broke along there! Some of the girls got caught.

My parents had a pony and trap. I was taking one of the U.S. soldiers and his girlfriend up the Beacon. They was a-snogging and I said, "Go on old boy."...to the horse!

MODEL FARM

My first wage, at Model Farm, was eight shillings and sixpence. There were no sprays so there were lots of thistles in the sheaves when we gathered them. We had to knock down the old boar thistles in the fields and we pulled the wild oats from the crop before it was cut. Then during the war the Ministry of Agriculture brought sprays round to the farms.

BUILDING THE COMBINE

Pam's father had one of the first combines. It came in boxes and had to be built at the farm. George Brown and Co., from Leighton Buzzard, supplied it and came to build it. There was the old man and three sons. Then it had to be filled with petrol. Then the business was near where Morrisons is now.

PRISONERS OF WAR

There were about ten to twelve German Prisoners-of-War picking potatoes and they were guarded by soldiers with guns.

PRODUCE FROM THE FARM

We were given cheese and butter and I always had a good bottle of milk from the farm. The best was 'the bisnings', (colostrum) – the second milk after calving. You poured it into a shallow dish, sweetened it and it thickened in the oven: delicious! We also had logs from the farm for heating and cooking on the kitchen range.

REARING OUR FOOD AT HOME

In summer, when we used to sell oil, we had a three burner stove outside. We kept just one pig. Dad had it slaughtered in Prestwood by Mr Stephens. We ate every bit of it – trotters, brawn, and faggots which were all the rough stuff. We had a big cockerel. We didn't let him run round much or he wouldn't get fat. We had him for Christmas. Nearly everyone had chickens and a couple or three cockerels in their backyard.

BROTHERS FOUGHT IN THE WAR

My oldest brother, Albert, was in India during the war. After VE Day he said "We'll get some tanks now!" (To fight the Japanese.) At the end of the war my other brother, Arthur, ended up in Germany.

VE DAY CELEBRATIONS

On VE Day, I joined the celebrations on Cheddington village Green where Sammy Chandler and Reg Bishop had a barrel organ to entertain everyone. I don't remember there being any food at these celebrations. Later I cycled up to Mentmore.

VE Day Celebration Day on the Green, Cheddington

The celebrations were held after VE day so that there
was time to organise the refreshments and games.

VE Day Celebration Day: Barrel Organ on The Green,
featuring Sammy Chandler (left) and Reg Bishop

Pam Mason

SCHOOL
I was just eight when war was declared and went to school, firstly in Old Bletchley, then at Brackley Hill School in Northampton and finally to Cedars Grammar School in Leighton Buzzard. I used to cycle down from Model farm to the Green to catch the bus to Leighton. In summer, if the weather was good, I used to cycle to Leighton because it was quicker.

MODEL FARM
My family, the Talbotts, took over the Model Farm in about 1940 when I was nine. It was about 1,000 acres. It started as 600 acres but then we added the other farm at West End. We had a dairy herd of Jerseys. We had a cowman who hand-milked about eight milkers. These were the Show cows. The rest were milked by machine.

A private firm took the milk to Northampton. We used to separate the cream. Mum used to make butter and the bread. There were always rabbits to eat and we kept about twenty pigs. We had one goose that chased everyone, chickens, turkeys and guinea fowl. I did quite a bit on the farm. I helped with hay-making by doing the mowing with the Fergie and at harvest time I collected the corn from the combine.

THE LAND GIRLS
There were five or six Land Girls working on the farm when there was lots to do like threshing the linseed. Three came from Wing. Some had lodgings, at the end of the war they stayed at the farm. There were also the estate workers.

We had five bedrooms so we were given two evacuees from Wandsworth, who stayed at the farm. They were Diane and Johnny Pluckrose. Their mother and father used to come down every fortnight, by train, and brought sweets. They used to walk across the field. Diane was between me and my sister Maisy, who was four years older than me, and Johnny was older than Maisy.

After the war my mother kept in touch with them and even visited Diane when she was working in a bank in Eastbourne, and my mother was in her eighties.

MY PONY
I had a small pony that my father bought for me, then later I had up to four horses.

Mrs Mary Ridpath had riding stables at Marsworth and the American soldiers used to ride there. She used to bring the ponies through the Bishop's fields to the water-works, then come up and round the Green and back again.

VE DAY
On VE Day I was at Mentmore where, at The Gas House there were sandwiches and jelly and cake for all the children, made by people using their ration coupons. During the war the Queen's golden coach was stored in Mentmore and George and I had the opportunity to sit in it!

M. Moss

GHENT — BELGIUM

COAL HOW PRECIOUS YOU WERE!

I'm going back to the year 1942 or 1943 during the occupation of Belgium, when my mama and myself were listening to the wireless, we heard a noise coming from the shed in our garden. Mama cried out: "Someone is stealing our coal!" Indeed some desperate boy (we did not think of him like that at the moment) had been shovelling what was left of our meagre ration of coal, into a sack, and had already succeeded to climb up the garden wall with one leg still dangling over the wall. Mama, my brave dear little mama, got hold of the creature's leg. He kicked and dropped our precious coal back on our side, all in the pitch darkness. He disappeared in a flash over the wall, and our coal was saved. It used to be so cold in the house that I used to warm my feet in our kitchen range and had to sleep in blankets as it was so cold in sheets.

EVERYTHING WAS IN SHORT SUPPLY

I remember cycling for miles to a farm to get a little extra watery milk and a little extra cheese on the "black market." Yes we did buy something on the "black market" because we were so hungry. We sold some household goods so we would be able (to buy) that little extra on the "black market" so frowned upon by our liberators who did not know what hunger was like.

MANY MEMORIES ARE FADING NOW

The last days of the German occupation when the German troops were retreating on their way out of the city a cannon was fitted on a railway carrier and bombarded in the city. As we lived near the railway we could hear the shells over the houses and explode nearby. Even then my mama would not join me in the cellar. "If I must die I die in my bed," she said.

I MET MY HUSBAND

We survived and were liberated on 6th September 1944, I met my lovely Englishman, a real gentleman, on 23rd September 1944 and thank God for many happy years together and four lovely children.

I LOVE ENGLAND

There is something else I would like to tell. When I came to England on the 2nd November 1945, having married my beloved RAF man on the 11th August, there were about six people travelling on a kind of landing craft. You could hear the sea lapping against the sides, we sat on deckchairs. From Folkestone by train to Victoria station. The hustle and the bustle of so many people, mostly military, was overwhelming. There I stood all by myself with my trunk and one suitcase and no one to greet me on the platform. I was sure my husband was waiting here to welcome me, but there was no one. I was approached. Suddenly a London policeman came up to me and after hearing my story told me not to talk to strangers and said "Just wait here. I'll stay with you." And for over three hours this wonderful guardian angel stayed with me on that platform. One of the happiest moments of my life was when suddenly I saw my Alan in his RAF blue overcoat running towards me. We flew into each other's arms and cried. Wherever he is, my most sincere and heartfelt thanks go to this wonderful policeman who delivered me safely into the arms of my beloved.

Dora McGuire

CHEDDINGTON

The war made for a good social life! The RAF and later the Americans were at the air base. Bombs were dropped at King's Head, Horton and Mentmore Road. The police were Air Raid Wardens. Colonel Shand Kydd was in charge of the Home Guard in Cheddington.

Ration coupons were a major part of the war years. £2 coupons were issued per person per year. These were to be used for food, clothes and other household goods. A coat cost 20 coupons while 2 were needed for stockings. As a consequence, jumble sales were popular. Jumpers were unpicked and re-knitted. Many things were in short supply. Blackout curtains had to be used but were not provided. Cars and bicycles had only tiny slivers of lights. Gas masks had to be carried everywhere together with identity cards. Ration books were still used in 1953, although clothes were no longer on ration.

Emily Bowles

EDGWARE

I was born in 1937 and lived in Edgware where I attended Stag Lane School. I can remember going into a shelter at school during air raids.

At home we had an Anderson Shelter in the garden but did not use it very often. Usually we sat under the dining room table during air raids. I thought this was a game!

My father was an electrician (a Reserved Occupation) and in the Home Guard.

I remember a large Street Party at the end of the war.

Brian Bowles

VE DAY

I had been evacuated twice during the war – to North Devon (with my mother) but on VE Day we were living back with my father at the family home at 28 Salehurst Road, Crofton Park, S.E. London.

There was a lot of excitement for an eight year old because of the talk of a 'Street Party'. We were, of course, hoping my brother would be coming home from Germany soon. He had enlisted and been through the first day of the D-Day Landings and been involved until the end.

I can remember Dad talking about being able to remove the Anderson Shelter from the garden.

Roger Hale

HOLLOWAY, NORTH LONDON

I was born in 1941 and spent the war years in Holloway, North London.

We had an Anderson Shelter in the back garden. I was not at school, being too young on VE Day, but I can vaguely remember my parents being elated.

FATHER DROVE BUSES FOR LONDON TRANSPORT

My father was invalided out of the Grenadier guards in 1942 and returned to his work as a London Transport Bus driver.

This, I believe, he was doing on VE day – driving his Number 29 bus from Southgate to Victoria.

John Halstead

JERUSALEM WEDDING
My parents met on a troop ship going round the Cape of Good Hope to the Middle East, where my father was in the RASC, providing supplies for the 8th Army, whilst my mother, a nursing sister in the QARNNS, helped operate on the wounded. They married in Jerusalem, then followed the action to Tunisia, Sicily and Caserta near Naples. By VE Day my mother was home with a 2 month old baby (me), and my father ready to return from Italy.

MAYORESS OF LONDON
During the Blitz my mother nursed at Barts, and her 'aristocratic' aunt (daughter of a horse dealer) was Lady Mayoress of London. Lady Coxen likes meeting the King and Queen, but disapproves of Churchill, who looked out of place in his scruffy boiler suit at the Mansion House. Lady Coxen lived to 107, feisty to the end.

Michael Davis

MUM A FIRE SPOTTER, DAD A POW
My mum was a Fire Spotter in London. Her family home in Sydenham was blown up by a V–bomb. My dad was a POW in Poland for five years and was rescued by the Russians.

Irene Johnson

PORTSMOUTH AND SIERRA LEONE
My father was posted on look–out duty on Pompey Hill, Portsmouth until it was realised that he was appallingly short-sighted.

He was then sent into the Merchant Navy and used to tell me tales of being chased by locals through the streets of Sierra Leone!

Bernadette Haysman

VE DAY
I remember coming out of school at four o'clock and the church bells ringing everywhere. My teacher told us, "You lucky children. You will never know what war is. Men have learnt."

During the war we did a lot of knitting to help the Red Cross and this still continued after VE Day.

There were a lot of foreign children in our school who had escaped, especially Jewish children, from danger.

Cynthia Needham

ROYAL ORDNANCE FACTORY, NOTTINGHAM
I was in the ATS. I went in at seventeen and a half and got free milk as I was under-age. I was in Nottingham, Chilwell, in the Royal Ordnance Factory. Lots of civilians were there too.

I used to drive Listers and Scammells, getting them ready for D-Day, and carrying parts to go to the stations.

On VE Day I was in York, at the Demob. Centre, issuing clothes to soldiers being demobbed. I saw lots of soldiers with limbs missing and serious injuries.

I was one of the last to be demobbed in September, 1945.

Molly Hodgskiss

(RHODA MARY ALLEN)

MR CHURCHILL

On VE Day I went to London and stood outside Buckingham Place. Mr Churchill passed and waved to us.

Les Steed

VE DAY

I was in The Bedfordshire and Hertfordshire Regiment, 21st Army Group HQ, as a driver.

On VE Day I drove officers from Monty's HQ to Brussels in a jeep. I had to hide the jeep in a pigsty just outside Brussels, so that I wouldn't lose it.

People were dancing in the street. Men in uniform, particularly British men, were mobbed, kissed and cuddled.

On the 7th May we took ceasefire dispatches to all different armies. (2nd Army, 5th Army) BLA - British Liberation Army.

Norbert Bybee

WISCONSIN, USA

VE DAY

I was eight years old. I remember being outside our house on Jones Street in Racine, Wisconsin.

The factory whistles started blowing and many passers-by had tears of joy in their eyes.

Jean Dumpleton

WIGGINGTON

I was four and a half years old at the start of the war and lived in Wigginton as a child. I remember being out playing as an eight year old and hearing V1 droning behind me, taking to my heels and running home in panic.

There were plenty of Americans about who used to throw chewing gum to children. In an area of Wigginton called The Flats. German and Italian Prisoners of War lived and worked though, as a young child, I was unaware of what their work was.

I recall eating a mash of condensed milk with bread and hot water for breakfast. As a child I asked my mother, "What happens when the war ends?" My mother told me that people would throw their hats in the air and jump in puddles.

I was in London, with relatives, when VE and VJ were celebrated and remember looking at the crowds in Trafalgar Square and wondering where the puddles were! People were joyous, singing and dancing.

I remember working with a man who had been a Prisoner of War who told me of being medically experimented on by the Germans. He suffered heart trouble thereafter.

Sometimes rear gunners were locked into their positions in the plane. Panic is known to have caused them to swivel their guns and shoot up the interior in error.

A Cheddington lad on the train, on a posting, wrapped a note around a brush and threw it out of the train to the crossing man who delivered a hint of his destination to the lad's parents.

Marjorie Connolley

I HAD A LOVELY WAR!

I had a lovely war. That may seem a strange statement, but as a child growing up in the country with my father at home, I was well protected from the horrors of war. I lived in Northchurch, with my family – mother, father and young sister. We had moved there in 1938 from South London when war was obviously a serious threat and we moved, also, to be near my grandparents.

FEW INCIDENTS

Although only about 30 miles from the centre of London, we were to the north, and so very rarely were there any incidents. I think there were two "doodlebugs", more technically known as V1s and V2s, which overshot London and landed harmlessly in fields, which caused great excitement and curiosity. There was also a light aircraft which crashed, again in a field, so you can see I had no understanding of what war was all about.

BUT A CROWDED HOUSE!

The main effect on my life was the number of visitors we had staying at the house – not all at the same time, and not for the duration of the war, but at times the house was pretty crowded for weeks on end. This must have been very trying for my parents, as the house was not big, but as all these visitors included children, my memories are of happy times and friendship. Who came? My mother's sister came to stay when her husband went into the army, and her baby was born in our house. Also my cousins Barbara and Margaret and their parents, and also their friends and their foster son, all came to escape the bombing in south London, and at one time we had two evacuees. They all came to us for relief from the bombing, and all of those children had experiences of the destruction of war from which I was protected. I have memories of my cousins diving under the table for the first few days of their visits whenever an aeroplane went over, until they got used to the safety of our home. School for me carried on as usual - their schooling was constantly interrupted.

FOOD

Food? Yes there was rationing, but we lived in the country, my father grew vegetables, we had fruit trees and bushes, we kept ducks for eggs and meat, we lived near the Common where we could gather mushrooms, raspberries, blackberries in season, and thanks to family in Dorset, we had a steady supply of rabbits sent to us through the post. Top of the list though, must be the fact that my mother was very good manager and cook.

END OF WAR BUT STILL NO BANANAS!

[At the end of the war] I have no memories of any celebrations or parties, just my disappointment of not being able to go immediately to the shop to buy bananas! I will explain: my mother had often said that when the war was over, the shops would be full of exotic goods that we had not been able to get during the war. As my memory of 'exotic' was bananas, I was very excited that my next trip to Berkhamsted would see me coming home with a banana. Not so for many months – or possibly years.

Horace Mason

OUR SHOP

At the beginning of the war I was at school. My brother Albert was soon called up to serve as an Acting Sergeant Major. I remember the Yanks – they used a building behind our shop to take radio messages, lots of Victor Romeo etc. The shop sold groceries, hardware, soap, pegs and other supplies. Apart from food, the other things were taken round with a horse and cart, and Albert helped my father. Paraffin was also sold, from a tank at the back. I got used to being a seller all my life - even at school, I would take things in to sell to my mates. I saved enough to buy my first car as soon as I was old enough to drive. It cost me forty-five pounds.

AIRCRASH AND BOMB

I remember an air crash on the Recreation Ground – the pilot had hit the lines above it. He was injured with a skinned arm. A bomb landed on the Mentmore Road, about 300 yards beyond the railway crossing and as boys we went to pick up shrapnel. We used our Anderson shelter behind the shop just once.

LIFE IN THE VILLAGE

We used the Reading Room a lot, the pool table, and it had newspapers and books, and we talked, and played cards. Gangs of us used to walk regularly, to the Beacon, and up to the Linces where we picked violets. We could take the train to Aylesbury or use bikes to get to Leighton Buzzard.

We had a child boarded with us when the evacuees came. We had Land Girls in the village - one very pretty one worked at Isaacs' fruit farm, packing fruit for sending to Brentford market. Dances and Whist Drives were organised by Mr Cleaver (Jack's Dad) and held at the Church Room in Station Road.

WORKING AT SEABROOK FARM

When I left school I worked for Mr Kingham at Seabrook Farm. I remember storing apples in the huge cellar under the house. I was also an ARP Messenger, ready to take messages from the ARP post near the Green to the School. I was exempt from the Army as a farm worker, although I would not have been called up as I had lost a finger when I was three.

Lewis Bonham

THE ROYAL ARTILLERY 8 CORPS

I spent VE Day in the army in The Royal Artillery 8 Corps in Germany on Luneburg Heath.

We started off at Normandy D-Day, plus we were offshore a long while waiting to get in (weeks!) We were battered about when the storm broke.

We were Sound Ranger Troops – listening for enemy guns firing and then we had to track them down and put our own artillery on them.

There were four to a crew and we felt vulnerable.

Sometimes you could see Germans walking about on the other side of fields.

FRACTURED THIGH

In Hanover on February 19th, 1945 I went over a bridge onto the railway line and fractured my thigh in an accident. I was in Hospital 603 in Hanover, then transferred back to hospital in Calais where I waited for the Hospital Boat to come back to Southampton: all in plaster!

I went in the Hospital Train to Pendlefield Hospital in Wakefield. When I got a bit better I was transferred to Hill End Hospital, St. Albans. I had the plaster off and convalesced at Bedford until 1947.

Mary Jones

PLENTY OF FOOD ON KENSWORTH FARM
Brought up on a farm at Church End, Kensworth.

Didn't really know there was a war on –

Plenty of milk, eggs – killed pigs, worked on farm.

Three girls all worked on the farm.

Had 5/- (five shillings) pay from Dad.

Later worked on a milk-round in Studham.

Mary Jones on the milk round at Studham

Pauline Pitman

PLYMOUTH

My family moved to Plymouth during the war as my mother thought as my father and brother were working in Plymouth, if they may have been killed we would all go down there to live so that we would all be together if we were bombed!

We all survived the Blitz and I remember listening to the different aircraft sounds as the English sea planes used to be based in Plymouth Harbour. The German aircraft used to follow them in and our sea planes used to fly round and round with the German aircraft following because our sea planes wouldn't try to land in the harbour.

I remember one of our school teachers was killed as her home was bombed. Of course we had barbed wire along the coastline everywhere and couldn't walk very far along the Barbican area because of the various destroyers, etc. which were moored along there.

We were used to seeing buildings which had been bombed and didn't seem to take a lot of interest as teenagers!

Rosemary Thorpe-Tracey

PLYMOUTH: FATHER VICAR OF ST MATTHEWS, STONEHOUSE

I was born in May 1936 so was three years old when war began in September 1939. I was then the fourth of five children (three boys and two girls); our youngest brother would follow in December 1941. My father was the vicar of St Matthews Church in Stonehouse, one of the three towns to make up the City of Plymouth. With the Devonport Naval Dockyard and the Millbay merchant docks, Plymouth was very much in the front line. It was severely bombed and the damage is said to have been proportionally as bad as Coventry.

Stonehouse was a tough dockside area and we lived on the Millbay Road alongside the Millbay Docks (which now serve the continental ferries), a prime target for the German bombers. The Royal Marine Barracks further down the road was near enough for us to hear reveille and 'lights-out,' and the Royal Marine band regularly marched past our house.

SHELTERING UNDER KITCHEN TABLE

I remember my mother would wake me up when the sirens sounded and carry me downstairs to the basement kitchen. I am even now gripped with fear if I wake up suddenly in the night. My eleven-year-old cousin Philip, who lived with us, having been evacuated from London, read to me as we sheltered under the kitchen table, terrified of the explosions of falling bombs and the racket of the guns firing all around us, from the barracks and docks and elsewhere.

Once we heard a strange rattle like the sound of tin cans falling down stairs and my mother calling frantically for my father who, with my elder brothers, went out on to the roof and kicked off the smouldering incendiaries before they exploded.

MY PARENTS HELPED THE HOMELESS

My father usually went out during the raids, wearing his helmet marked with a white cross, to do what he could for people bombed out of their homes. And afterwards both my parents would help in rest centres set up for the homeless.

Years later I met someone who remembering them told me, "He was always out, when the bombs were coming down, helping the people. He and his wife, too, always helping the people."

MOTHER'S PREMONITION SAVES US

Eventually we slept in the dining room next to the kitchen but suddenly one night my mother had a premonition which made her rush in and drag us quickly from our beds and out of the room. Within seconds the blast from bombs falling on the town hall behind the house blew the windows across our beds.

OUR FLIGHT FROM PLYMOUTH

It must have been then, the spring of 1941, when my parents decided that my sister, Marigold, who was eight, and I should be sent out of Plymouth. I have a surreal memory of our flight that evening when the air-raid, which turned out to be one of the most devastating, just got started. My memory is of a strangely empty double-decker bus carrying the conductor, my sister and me and a solitary man in a trilby hat. As we sped along I was terribly sick and the man in the trilby cleaned me up with a large white handkerchief. Marigold, though, remembers the event somewhat differently. Still indignant, she says that it was a packed *single-decker,* that it was she who cleaned me up, with the large white handkerchief given to her by the man in the trilby, that the people nearby complained loudly and that she had been very embarrassed!

EXCITING PLYMOUTH

Later when the blitz came to an end, Plymouth, though in ruins, was a pretty exciting place. The Sound bristled with battleships, cruisers, destroyers – all kinds of vessels. Sea-planes landed and took off. Because the row of houses opposite had been bombed we could see into the docks where so much was going on. We saw the waiting barges for D-Day and when one morning they had disappeared we knew they were heading for the Normandy beaches. It is only recently that I learnt they carried the Bailey bridges used in the landings.

THE AMERICANS

Plymouth was packed with troops and friendly and generous American GIs were all over the place. Sometimes they were a bit too friendly and generous, giving my father the extra work in tracking down the fathers of the numerous babies born in the parish. We had a GI of our own, Sergeant Stone, who appeared whenever we visited our favourite beach to share our simple picnic with his offerings of peanut butter, fruit cake and other exotic goodies. Mother

invited him to tea one day and we were very sad that he was suddenly posted and could not come. He wrote to apologise but as we never heard from him again we felt he must have been killed.

BANANAS FROM A NAVAL CAPTAIN!

After Evensong my parents would gather up any servicemen in the congregation and bring them home for supper. So Sunday evenings were often pretty lively with soldiers, sailors and airmen of all ranks filling up our sitting-room. Once a naval captain who had been away a long time turned up and as my mother greeted him at the door he said, "I have a present for you" and pulled from his jacket a bunch of very green bananas. Such joy – the first time I had seen bananas.

ONE PENNY TO VISIT THE U-BOAT!

Towards the end of the war we learnt that a U-Boat had been captured and was berthed in the Millbay dock. Walking home from school on my own one afternoon I wandered over to the berth. There were several other children milling around and the naval rating on guard duty, in the spirit of private enterprise, let us all down into the boat charging us 1d each. I was about nine-years-old and the freedom that children had then is astonishing when compared with attitudes today. I found the submarine to be a pretty horrid place, small, cramped with a dreadful smell. I did get to play with the periscope, though, and I wonder how many people can say that they have looked up the periscope of a German U Boat.

Joan Ward

ARMY CAMPS AROUND SALISBURY PLAIN

My most vivid memories have to be those of the war years, 1939 – 1945. I was a child of seven when the war broke out. I lived in Andover, in Hampshire, where we were very much aware of what was happening.

The town seemed to be surrounded by troops of many nationalities. There were huge numbers of Army camps spread out as far as Salisbury Plain to the west and Winchester to the east. There was an Air Force base at Thruxton, just outside Andover, and twenty miles to the south was the Navy and the Docks at Southampton.

ANTI-GERMAN FEELING

Southampton was a target for the German bombers and the attacks there were relentless and sometimes we could see the glow in the sky from the fires after a raid. We were too far inland and saw very little enemy activity although the sound of hundreds of bombers, night after night, was a sound one would never forget. A German aircraft did crash in our area and four airmen were killed. There was great controversy in the town as to where these men should be buried. Some people felt that they should not be given a Christian burial. However, humanity won the day and they were buried in the cemetery of the Parish Church. One has to remember that anti-German feeling was very strong at that time – almost to the point of hatred.

WITNESSED PREPARATION FOR D-DAY

Of course, the close proximity of Andover to Southampton meant that we were just in the right place for the troop build-up in preparation for D-Day. I remember standing, with lots of other children, on a bridge, which was called 'The Iron Bridge,' which crossed the main road from Andover to Winchester and Southampton. We watched the continual stream of lorries carrying troops to, what I now know to be, embarkation for D-Day. These convoys of troops went on for days.

THE AMERICANS ARRIVE

The American arrived in 1942 and were like a breath of fresh air. They were smart, cheerful and very generous.

PRISONER OF WAR CAMPS

We also had Prisoner of War camps in the area. Some of the Germans were put to building roads. One of these roads was where I later lived when I was first married.

One particular group, who became familiar to us, were all German soldiers except one who was a sailor. He had a beautiful singing voice and he would start them singing and they would all join in. They seemed reasonably happy, no doubt glad to be finished with fighting.

There was also an Italian POW camp but I did not have contact with any of these. I seem to remember that they were not particularly liked by local people.

Among the troops were a number of different nationalities; in particular, we did seem to have a lot of Polish troops, again, not especially liked by the locals.

SCHOOLS

Because of the continual air raids in Southampton, the Grammar School children here were brought into Andover to share that school. Southampton children had the school for half the day and the Andover children had the other half. The system seemed to work fairly satisfactorily.

RATIONS

These were, of course, very meagre but we did not fare too badly. Everyone tried to grow some vegetables and people did seem to store what they had and I cannot remember going hungry. We had one egg per week per person. Meat was in very short supply. The meat ration was not sold by weight but by price, so if you bought a cheap joint you got more for your money. Most people could not afford meat every day and one of my favourite dishes was a pie made with vegetables only. There was no tinned food available, no bananas or oranges. At Christmas time the Merchant Navy, who risked their lives to bring in food supplies, tried very hard to bring in some oranges so that children could have a Christmas treat. During the war, all children were given free milk at school and young mothers were given orange juice or rose hip syrup for babies. We were also given cod liver oil, but I am not sure if this was free. Every morning I would be given a spoonful of this stuff, which I absolutely hated.

FEEDING MY DOG WITH HORSEMEAT

We had a little dog but during the war lots of people put their pets down simply because there was not enough food for them. One of my jobs was to go into town, on a Saturday, to a horse butcher who supplied horsemeat for dogs. This meat was unfit for human consumption and was painted with green paint.

The smell in that little shop was atrocious. I did not enjoy going there.

CHRISTMAS

There were few luxuries at Christmas. The toys we received were usually second-hand and very simple: perhaps a colouring book and a few pencils, or a jigsaw puzzle. Generally we had to make our own amusement. A shoebox can be used to make all sorts of things with the help of old wooden cotton reels, bits of string etc. It did teach us to use our imagination.

The Americans were great and made such a fuss of the children. We were invited to parties at various halls in the town, or out to the army camps where we were fed and entertained. I remember one invitation, in particular, which was for a cooked lunch. We were given a huge plate on which there was meat with gravy and vegetables, including sweet corn.

The Americans held a Christmas party for children from Cheddington, Long Marston and Marsworth, December 1944

This was something we had never had before. For us, maize was something you fed only to chickens. On the same plate we had a large slice of cherry pie, complete with custard. Gravy and custard doesn't taste too bad if you are hungry. This was followed by a large, one pint tin mug full of cocoa. It was surprising that we were not all sick after that. When we left to go home we all staggered under tins of food, boxes of biscuits, cakes, and enough sweets to last for months. They were so kind and generous and loved entertaining the children. To us, they were real heroes.

THE GERMAN POWs MADE TOYS FOR US
The German POWs, too, showed their human side and made some lovely wooden toys:, doll's houses, trucks etc. which were hand-painted with lovely floral patterns, and these were given to local children.

WASTE NOT WANT NOT
I think my wartime memories have had a very lasting effect on my life. We learned to appreciate things and to take nothing for granted. We tried not to waste food. The war years were very hard ones in many ways but a lot of good came out of it too.

Sheila Morton, nee Parkins

AT HOME: UNDER THE STAIRS FOR AIR RAIDS
I was five when the war started and eleven when it ended. Mum used to get us up when there was an air raid. There was a cupboard under the stairs with a mattress in it. There were searchlights, blackout curtains upstairs and an outside toilet blacked out with a lino 'cage frame'. Once, during very bad bombing I had whooping cough.

AT SCHOOL: IN THE SHELTER WITH BARLEY SUGAR
I was at George Street School in Hemel Hempstead. When the air raid siren went we lined up to go down to the shelter at the back of the school with our gas masks and we were given a stick of barley sugar to keep us quiet!

In July 1944 a bomb went off in Mimm's Field, adjacent to St. Paul's, and killed a horse.

SOLDIERS FLY TO ARNHEM IN GLIDERS
One Sunday morning poor soldiers were put into gliders, and planes pulled them to Arnhem. Hundreds flew over Hemel - the sky was full of them.

FOOD LIMITED
Our food was very limited and my parents struggled to put food on the table.

THE AMERICANS ARRIVE!
Then the Americans came. A husband came home from the navy and his wife was entertaining an American. The American jumped out of the window and the woman threw his trousers out of the window after him.

I took years to work out why she threw his trousers out!

Trevor A Chrich

JUST ONE ON VE DAY!

I can't remember, having only just had my first birthday the day before! But I was with my mother who lived with her parents in Nottingham.

THE CALL UP

My father was born in 1920, and so was only 19 when the Second World War broke out. He worked for the local electricity company, and so was in a "reserved occupation." That meant that he was not likely to be called up to fight in the war. There were lots of other "reserved occupations" including coal-miners, farmers, teachers and doctors. The Government thought that these workers were essential to keep the country running properly in time of war.

But many of the young men who were in reserved occupations wanted to join up to fight the enemy. There were lots of reasons: sometimes because their friends had joined up, or had been called up to join the armed forces, other times because those young men who were not in uniform were regarded as inferior, because they were unfit to be soldiers, or because they were "conscientious objectors." These were people whose beliefs – religious or otherwise – meant that they did not believe in fighting wars to settle disputes between nations. They were nicknamed "conshies" and were often hated by other people whose sons, husbands or boyfriends had gone away to fight.

MY FATHER JOINS THE ARMY

So my father decided that he wanted to join the Army. In 1941 he joined a new regiment called the 22nd Dragoons. They operated tanks which were the Army's chief fighting weapon of the war. Because the regiment was new, it spent most of the war training to fight, and they didn't get to do any fighting before 6th June 1944 when the Allied Forces invaded France, which had been overrun and occupied by the Germans.

CLEARING THE BEACHES IN NORMANDY

On 6th June 1944 the mighty invasion force of British, American and Canadian forces crossed the English Channel to land on beaches in Normandy. My father's regiment was responsible for clearing the beaches of mines which had been placed as defences to blow up anyone who tried to invade from the sea. To do that, his tank had a "flail" on the front – like a huge bobbin of spinning chains. The idea was that the chains would detonate the mines well in front of the tank so that the soldiers could follow behind without getting into danger.

INJURED - AND THEN THREE YEARS IN HOSPITAL

My father's war lasted only 7 days. On the night of 13th June 1944 a German Stuka dive-bomber dropped bombs on his unit. The bombs were anti-personnel mines, which, when they exploded, sent millions of little bits of metal called "shrapnel" flying in all directions. My father tried to take cover by hiding under a tank, but the left side of his body was hit by lots of shrapnel and he was very badly wounded in his left arm and left leg. He was treated in a "field hospital" in Normandy, and then was flown back to England where he spent the next three years in hospital.

Jose Cockrem

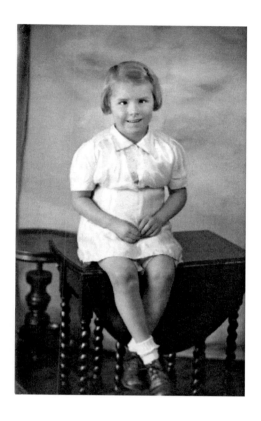

FATHER HEAD GARDENER AT THE MANOR

I moved with my parents namely Ernest and Lily Cockrem to Cheddington the year before the outbreak of the Second World War, when my father took up the position of Head Gardener at Cheddington Manor.

Both of my parents were from the north of England, and we'd been living at Corsham in Wiltshire, where my father had been employed as Under Gardener to Colonel C Nicholson on his Hartham Park Estate. Moving to Cheddington meant that my mother could see more of her London relatives. My aunt and uncle, namely Phoebe and Bill Webster, had a small car in which they would drive down from London to see us at weekends.

WAR DECLARED

On Sunday, 3rd September 1939 war was declared. From then onwards everyone had to be seen to be doing something towards the war effort.

HOME GUARD

My father was enlisted into the local Home Guard Unit, which was run by his employer, namely Mr Lawrence Bowring Stoddart, who ultimately attained the rank of Captain, and Colonel Norman Shand Kydd, who lived at Horton Hall. Guarding the home front meant that you worked in your normal employment during the daytime and went on guard during the night. I have vague recollections of my father returning home during the early hours of the morning after a night on guard.

WOMEN KNITTED SOCKS FOR SOLDIERS

Mrs Stoddart organized a women's knitting class, which met at Cheddington Manor and was known as 'Knitting Socks for Soldiers'. These women knitted socks and balaclava helmets for the soldiers.

AIR RAID PRECAUTIONS

Mr Harold Perry, who lived in a house overlooking The Green, was the Air Raid Precautions (ARP) Warden. Mr Reginald Tompkins, the local undertaker, was a Special Constable, assisting the village 'bobby' with his duties.

WESTEND HILL OBSERVATION POST

The Royal Observer Corps had an observation post in Westend Hill, which was manned by men from the village, one of whom was Mr Frank Jeffery, Head Master at Cheddington School.

NATIONAL SAVINGS

Every man, woman and child was encouraged to save money towards the war effort. The National Savings Advertisement, which appeared in the newspapers, contained a foreboding animal, called the 'Squander Bug'. He was to make sure that you put some money into National Savings each week towards the 'War Effort'. Mrs Phoebe Alcock the village Sub Post-mistress, Mrs Margaret Towell, and the school were designated to promote National Savings.

Both Mrs Alcock and Mrs Towell would collect money from the residents and issue savings stamps, which were affixed to a book. When you had enough stamps in your book, you could purchase a Savings Certificate, earning you a good rate of interest if you did not cash it within five years. Pupils took a minimum of sixpence per week to school to buy savings stamps with the incentive to buy savings certificates.

REST CENTRE FOR BOMBED-OUT HOMELESS

The Methodist Church Schoolroom was designated a Rest Centre for people from London, who had lost their homes in bombing raids, and was equipped with folding beds, which stood up against the walls in readiness.

GAS MASKS

It was feared that the Germans would use 'gas warfare' against the British population, so every man, woman and child was issued with a 'Gas Mask'. Babies had a pink one, with two round windows to see out of, which was known as a 'Mickey Mouse' Gas Mask. Children and adults had a black gas mask with a window almost the width of the mask for see out of. Services personnel were issued with a 'respirator', which was heavier than the civilian ones. When it was feared there would be a 'gas attack' you had to carry your gas mask with you wherever you went, i.e. school, work, etc.

THE BLACKOUT

Every window in your house was fitted with blackout blinds so the enemy could not see a community from the sky after dark. The lower half of a front cycle light had to be blacked out too.

PREPARING FOR EVACUEES FROM LONDON

The Billeting Officer assessed each home for the intake of evacuees from London, allocating them as he saw fit. Many evacuees from London came to live in Cheddington and attended the village school.

WIMPEY'S BUILD CHEDDINGTON AERODROME

Farmers' fields were requisitioned for war work, enabling the construction of Cheddington Aerodrome, which stretched from behind West End and South End Linces to Long Marston and Marsworth with the main runway stopping short of Cooks Wharf. Initially the aerodrome, which was constructed by Wimpey's, became home to a squadron of the Royal Air Force.

THE CALL-UP

During the early part of the war, men from the village were gradually being called to active service, the younger ones first and the older ones later on. One man opted to join the 'Bevin Boys' and worked in a coal mine. At least one young woman served in the Land Army. Some of the young men were married and had started a family, their wives being left to bring up their children. Young men were sent to the Far East, and those who had children didn't see them again until they were demobilized at the end of the war. One father was drafted to the Far East, when his wife was pregnant with their second child, and did not see their son until he was five years old.

MY FATHER GUARDED THE COAST

My father was called-up about two years into the war. As he was an older soldier, he was placed on coastguard duty in this country, first at Cromer in Norfolk, then in the Orkney Islands guarding Scapa Flow. I was fortunate, because he was able to come home on leave, especially on compassionate grounds when I was very ill in hospital following a tonsillectomy, which went wrong. I recollect my father coming home on his first leave, and hiding behind the settee, because I didn't recognize him as being my father. My mother persuaded me to come out of hiding as this man in uniform was my father.

VISITING MY FATHER

When my father managed to get leave in the summer holidays, my mother and I would meet him in Yorkshire, where we would spend a week with my grandmother. We travelled to the north of England, first visiting my maternal grandfather in Cheshire. The next week, we would travel to Yorkshire on the Pennine Railway to meet up with my father. The trains were full and we often had to sit on our suitcase, keeping an eye on the smaller one, which contained our rations.

Ernest Cockrem

POSTED TO BRITISH LIBERATION ARMY

When the German Army was in retreat, my father was posted to the British Liberation Army, which later became the British Army of the Rhine. During this period, we received letters from him, but we were not allowed to know where he was. After demobilization, we learnt that he had helped with the liberation of Arnhem and had finished his service in Germany. We also learnt that during his time in Arnhem, he had been wounded by a booby trap. The medical team managed to save his eye and he was able to move on with his regiment. I gather that when he was stationed in Germany, my father was involved in guarding

Prisoner of War Camps, which housed Germans whom we had taken prisoner, and Displaced Persons Camps, which housed many nationalities of people who had become displaced through the war.

RESERVED OCCUPATIONS

The government classed certain employments as essential or reserved occupations, which meant that their work was vital to the war effort. People so engaged may not be called to active service. Locally essential/reserved occupations were agriculture, the railway and the canal. Factories were turned over to war work and Gossards in Leighton Buzzard, which made brassieres and corsets, was commissioned to manufacture 'Barrage Balloons', which meant girls employed by them would not be called into the services.

RATIONING

The war brought rationing - everything was rationed including coal, food, sweets, soap, clothing, shoes, and household linen. Commodities had to be made to a wartime standard so clothing, shoes, sheets, blankets and furniture bore the utility mark. Food rationing did not bring starvation to the population. We had at least two meals every day – breakfast and lunch/dinner. For breakfast, streaky bacon stretched further than any other! For lunch/dinner extras such as a rabbit were always welcome. My mother would skin a rabbit, get it ready for the 'pot', and cook it. When we had guests my mother collected their surplus ration coupons to buy tea and soap, also clothing and shoes for me. Women, whose husbands were in the armed forces, took over their husband's allotments. My mother worked my father's allotment, so we were never short of vegetables. The coal allowance was often supplemented by wood from Mentmore Spinneys, which had broken off the trees. My mother used my pram to get it home. Most people cooked their meals on a solid fuel kitchen range, which would also burn wood. Towards the end of the war, our sheets were thin and well patched. I recollect going with my mother to a Ministry Office in Leighton Buzzard in the hope of getting some sheet dockets. She was refused, so she put up a case to the man at the desk, suggesting that if he didn't grant her some dockets, I would have to lie in a bed without sheets, which wouldn't be very nice for a child. He gave her some dockets and we had new sheets.

POOR PAY IN THE SERVICES

Services pay fell far short of the weekly wage which a person had been receiving from their employment. A married man was required to allocate an allowance from his pay to his wife and child/children. This would be drawn weekly by his wife at the Post Office. There were many instances where a man had a widowed mother to support, so I assume that he could make over an allowance to her. Dependants of service personnel were also given the perquisite of quarter fare on the railway.

THE AIRMEN ARRIVE: RAF THEN AMERICANS

Early occupants of Cheddington Aerodrome were British Airmen, who frequented the village dances, and dated the local girls. Dances were also held on the camp.

In 1944, two million American servicemen were drafted into Great Britain for training to help us in pushing the German Army into retreat, so as to liberate the occupied countries of Europe. Subsequently, the British airmen were posted elsewhere and the aerodrome became an American Military Base. We were soon aware that the 'Yanks' had arrived! They rode their large bicycles through the village and sat on The Green in their leisure time. The 'Yanks' had more money to spend than British servicemen. You could say that they were 'overpaid' and 'over here!' During licensing hours, the pubs were full to capacity! They frequented the village dances, and courted the village girls, three of whom became 'GI Brides'. The boys used to ask the Yanks "Have you got any gum chum?" The message was received by their commanding officer, who sent a large box of sweets to the school. This was most welcome, because every pupil had some extra sweets that week.

COUSIN CAMERON LEAVES LONDON

When London was threatened with bombing raids, my aunt and uncle brought Cameron, my cousin who was about 10 years old, to Cheddington to be looked after by my parents, because they wanted him to be safe. He went to the village school, and made friends with the village boys and girls. To him this experience was a great adventure! On account of petrol rationing, his parents had to use public transport to visit him. Cameron's half-brother, 18 years his senior, was married and serving in the Royal Navy. During the bombing raids, my aunt and uncle slept on Tooting Broadway Underground Station every night, so coming to Cheddington was a relaxation.

When there was a lesser threat of bombs being dropped, Cameron returned to London to finish his education. He had lived in Cheddington for about two-and-half years.

WE TOOK IN GUESTS FROM ROSEBERY ARMS

To supplement her income my mother, who held the rank of housekeeper, took in the overflow of guests from the Rosebery Arms Hotel. These were mostly women, who were in the services and had men friends stationed on the aerodrome. This casual occupation lasted for about two years.

VISITS FROM OUR FAMILY IN LONDON

When there were no guests staying with us, my aunt, uncle and Cameron would pay us a weekend visit. In those days the majority of people didn't have telephones in their homes, so you communicated by letter or telegram. To send a telegram, you gave your message to the Post Office during normal working hours. My aunt would write to my mother indicating that they would be coming for the weekend, but not always! They would catch the last train from London, which arrived in Cheddington at approximately nine o'clock.

My mother, who had exceptional hearing, would listen for the train coming into the station and allow half-an-hour for them to arrive. If they didn't come by 9.30pm we would get ready for bed.

Members of the Women's Army Auxiliary Corps arrive at Cheddington in 1944 from Stone Replacement Depot.

Men of the 2901st CCRC Group sit around the stove that provided the warmth. The boxes on the floor provided heat in another form: chilli con carne. These men were the first Americans to arrive at Cheddington.

OUR HOUSE A RETREAT FOR BOMB VICTIMS

On a Saturday evening during the summer of 1944, we waited until about 9.30pm as usual and gave up on them by 9.45. In those days we had two hours of British Summer Time, known as 'double summer time', so it was daylight until after 11pm. Our house was a few doors away from the Methodist Church. Around 10 o'clock, I looked out of our front window and saw a group of people coming round the corner of The Green by the 'Old Inn Public House'. I said "Mummy there's some people coming round the corner – look there's Cameron!" But who were the others? Eventually my mother opened our front door to be confronted with a line of people standing on our garden path. My uncle Bill did the 'spiel!' "Lily, we're bombed out!" "A Doodle Bug hit us last night!" My mother invited everyone into our home. There were nine adults, one baby and a dog!! They were my Aunt Phoebe, Uncle Bill and Cameron, together with their neighbours Will and Joan Cobham, Mrs Bowles (Joan's mother), who was well into her 80's, Mr & Mrs Scott, their dog, and Flossie Dewar carrying a small baby in her arms. They had stopped at the Rosebery Arms for a drink, my uncle, telling everyone "We've been bombed out!"

THE MEN TAKE OVER THE METHODIST CHURCH

My mother was now faced with a dilemma, because she hadn't enough beds for all of these people, and would not let anyone sleep on the floor. She had a brainwave! The Methodist Church Schoolroom was designated as a Rest Centre and there was a need to use it. She would accommodate the women and the baby, but not the men and the dog, which on their way from the station ran into the road and nearly got tangled up in a Yank's bicycle wheel. My mother got permission for the men to use the Schoolroom, provided our guests would vacate it in time for Sunday School the following morning. Cameron joined the men and this was his version of events. Thankful to be alive, they were on a high! His father, who was a good party entertainer, rose to his 'Burlington Bertie' Act, using the chapel poker as a walking stick. 'Scotty' (Mr Scott) ascended the pulpit and pretended to preach to his flock! Afterwards everyone chatted about the day's events before settling down in the hope of getting a night's sleep! I think that this was the only occasion on which the Rest Centre was used, and this was unofficial!

FLOSSIE'S PARENTS KILLED BY BOMB

Later, the story unfolded, a Doodle Bug (V1/V2 self-propelled rocket) had hit Links Road during the early hours of Saturday morning. Flossie, who lived on the opposite side of the road to the others, had lost her home and her parents. When the air raid siren sounded, Flossie carrying her baby managed to get to the public air raid shelter, but her parents did not and were killed. The houses in which the other people lived (including my aunt and uncle) were badly shattered with ceilings down, windows cracked and dust everywhere. Scrambling for cover, my aunt had fallen down the steps of the Anderson Air Raid Shelter, which they now had in their back garden. She had received First Aid, but no proper medical attention. Fortunately, my mother had kept my cot, pram and nappies, which were useful for the baby. I cannot recollect how she managed to feed all of these people and the dog! Perhaps some had salvaged their rations.

On the Monday morning, my mother called in Doctor Square from Leighton Buzzard to attend to my aunt's injured leg, which left her slightly handicapped. Flossie returned to London with the men on Sunday evening. They had to go to work and she had formalities to complete in connection with her Mother and Father's deaths. I don't know what emergency arrangements were made for Flossie and her baby, or if there were relatives in London, who could support her. Later Flossie and her little boy came to stay with us, pending the go-a-head to take up residence with her parents-in-law in the Midlands. I have recollections of my mother helping Flossie bath her baby in front of the fire, and talking to her most of the time. Flossie's was one of those hasty wartime marriages! 'You lived for today.' 'You didn't worry about the future!' She had met and married a serving soldier before he was sent abroad, their baby possibly being conceived on his embarkation leave. Had her husband been stationed in this country he would have been allocated a few days compassionate leave, but no more than that! My mother claimed two shillings and sixpence (12.5 pence) each from the government for accommodating my aunt, Mrs Bowles, Flossie and her son during their stay with us.

VILLAGE TEACHER LOSES PARENTS TO BOMB

In those days, the Headmaster at Cheddington School lived in the School House, which was adjacent to the school. Miss Winifred Alderman, a young teacher came from High Wycombe. During term time she lodged with Mr & Mrs Hignett and spent the weekends and holidays with her family in High Wycombe. She travelled into Aylesbury, transferring to either train or bus to get home. One Friday evening, Miss Alderman walked to the station as usual, and was met at the by a policeman, who told her not to proceed with her journey, because her parents had been killed by a bomb that day. From then onwards, Miss Alderman lived with Mr Jeffery & Mrs Jeffery (Headmaster and his wife), who treated her as a daughter. She lived with them until her marriage to Mr Bill Soul in 1948. I last saw Mrs Soul at Miss Doris Beilby's funeral in 1991. I gather that she died in the mid -2000s.

THE YANKS LEAVE CHEDDINGTON

At the end of the war, the 'Yanks' moved out of Cheddington, and the aerodrome returned to being a British Air Force Base. The American Servicemen returned to America for demobilization. Those who married had to leave their wives, and in some cases a child, behind. During the year after the war ended, the three G.I. Brides (one with her small daughter) sailed to America on one of the ships, which were commissioned to reunite the brides with their husbands.

WALKING ROUND THE LINCES

In those days, members of the public were allowed to walk round the Linces. Access was through a kissing gate at the side of the entrance, which led to 'Keeper's Cottage', now known as 'Falcon House'. 'Keeper's Cottage' was so named, because it was the home of the gamekeeper who was employed by the Earl of Rosebery on the Mentmore Estate. In the summer, you could pick violets and primroses, which grew in the wooded area. You could see the crews preparing the aeroplanes for the night's sortie. My mother would often take me for a walk round the Linces, which made for a pleasant afternoon out. She would also take me on a round trip down to Cooks Wharf,

along the canal towing path to Brownlow Bridge, returning along the Ivinghoe Road via Cheddington Station, then up to the village. We would also walk along the towing path to Marsworth, returning the way we went.

ROYAL COACH

During one of our walks to Mentmore, I recollect sitting in one of the royal coaches, either the Gold State Coach or the Irish State Coach, which had been evacuated from the Royal Mews near to Buckingham Palace and stored in a building at the bottom of Gas House Hill (on the road leading to Wing). My mother knocked on the door of the house and asked Lord Rosebery's employee, who lived there, if I could see the Royal Coach and he took us into the building to see it. The interior was crimson velvet and I felt like a princess sitting there.

VE DAY AND VJ DAY

I recollect VE Day as being a normal one. The previous evening someone went around the village telling parents not to send their children to school, as tomorrow had been declared a national holiday. I don't recollect any celebrations in Cheddington for either this or VJ Day (we may have been in the north of England on VJ Day).

GENERAL ELECTION

Soon after VE Day, the wartime coalition government decided to hold a General Election. As a child I wondered what it was all about with blue, yellow and red posters displayed in residents' windows together with photographs of the candidates representing each of the three main political parties (Conservative, Liberal and Labour). The three candidates also held 'open air' meetings at The Green. Mr Aidan Crawley, Socialist Labour Party, commonly known as the Labour Party, became our Member of Parliament on 5th July, 1945.

FATHER DEMOBBED

Once the war was over, family life started returning to a degree of normality as men were gradually being demobilized from the Armed Forces. My father was released from the Royal Artillery in 1946. I recollect the day my father came home on demobilization leave. My mother had known for several weeks that he was likely to be 'demobbed', but the exact date had not been given him. It was a case of waiting for the day! There were no 'flags or bunting' to welcome him home. I went to school as normal. When I came home at lunchtime, my father was sat in a chair in our living room. He had been 'demobbed' at Northampton and returned home during the morning. I also recollect that upon demobilization he was given new clothes and a gratuity of about £60 to set himself up in 'Civvy Street'

CLOSE KNIT COMMUNITY

During the 'War Years', Cheddington was a 'close-knit community', with everyone pulling together to help each other!

MOTHER PICKED FRUIT

Towards the end of the war, several of the women encouraged my mother to take up seasonal work as a Fruit Picker. She jumped at this opportunity to earn some extra money, which helped to finance our annual visits to Cheshire and Yorkshire. This was the only time I saw my grandparents. Her first employment was with Aldridge's of High Wycombe. They used to buy the fruit crop as a 'job lot', this was in the orchards on the north side of Long Marston Road and Station Road and possibly some in Horton. Prior to the fruit picking season Mr Jack Vickers and Mr Jack Day from Aldridge's would come to the village and engage their workers. Later she worked for Mr Arthur Reed (Dora McGuire's uncle), who had orchards in Cheddington and Pitstone, and Mr Godfrey Isaacs at Church Hill Farm. The land on the northerly edge of Church Hill Farm was arable land, upon which he used to grow potatoes, so his work continued into November with potato picking.

During the war and early in the post war years, I recollect seeing German prisoners of war working at Church Hill Farm.

CHRISTMAS 1945 IN THE DEVASTATED LONDON

My mother and I spent the first Christmas 1945 with my aunt and uncle in London. I recollect the devastation, which the 'Doodle Bug' had caused! There was no Health and Safety fencing around the ruined houses, so Cameron and I were able to have a close look at what was left! The top storey had gone! In one ruin, you could see a wash basin hanging onto the part of a wall, which hadn't collapsed. The ceilings were still down in my aunt and uncle's home. You could see wood hanging from the laths and plaster ceilings. My aunt and uncle were still waiting for the War Damage Commission to assess their claim. Despite this we had a good Christmas. This was the first time, that I had seen my uncle entertaining as 'Burlington Bertie!'

AERODROME FIELDS RETURNED TO FARMERS

In the years after the war, the fields which had been requisitioned for building the Aerodrome were gradually returned to the farmers.

FRY'S CHOCOLATE BARS

Throughout the war, my father would save up his NAAFI rations, so I had a supply of 'Fry's Chocolate Bars', when he came home on leave.

NOTES: 1. During the war years and for many years afterwards, Cheddington Aerodrome was definitely known as such and not Cheddington Airfield. 2. The Chapel and the Schoolroom were heated by large cast iron coke-burning stoves.

Pat Banister

CREATON

We lived in a small village, Creaton, nine miles north of Northampton and amazingly one night two doodlebugs found us, short of their destination of Coventry. I remember going to my primary school the following morning to get *the* bottle of milk (something we all had every school day up to the 1950s) and seeing not only the school roof partly missing but more impressively a row of bungalows with no roofs at all. I can still clearly picture this awful sight.

Joyce Mullet

STREET PARTY ON VE DAY

I remember having a street party on VE Day. I was living in Wimbledon and the rationing was bad. The war was very boring for civilians as we were not able to do much until the war ended.

SICK HUSBAND

My husband worked on the Southern Railway but went to war. Within a year he was an invalid due to having rheumatic fever. He was in hospital a long time recovering from this illness.

SON FOUND IN GUTTER

I had a cousin living in Worthing and their son went to Scotland as an evacuee. The family worried so much about him they went to visit him. They found him playing in the gutter and brought him back home.

Connie Kingshott

FIRST HUSBAND

I met my first husband when he was in a military band. He worked in a factory as a stonemason. In the war he was billeted to Henley on Thames and was sent to Italy. He was not there long when I got a telegram to say he had been injured. He had been caught in some cross fire and died a few days later. We had been married two years but had been together for only three weeks, in short leaves, in all that time.

MARRIED AGAIN

I married again and my second husband was taken prisoner of war at Dunkirk but he was released because he lost his hand.

BLACKOUT

At home all the curtains were lined with blackout material and when the siren went, I went in a cupboard under the stairs.

MUSIC WHILE YOU WORK

I worked in a tool room at Stewart and Tanners. Special playtime music was put on mainly for factory workers.

Karen Boddy

Karen was a past Chairman of Cheddington History Society. Sadly she died in 2007.

PARENTS MEET ON VE DAY

My parents met on VE Day in Scarborough. My mother was a student teacher, and her friend knew one of the soldiers stationed in the town. As the soldiers (Royal Engineers) walked past the windows of the Teacher Training College, which had been moved to Scarborough from Leeds, my mum and her friend leaned out to wave to them. They were reprimanded for waving at soldiers!

Later that evening my parents met formally.

Dorothy Morris

Dorothy is Karen's mother, and these are extracts from her memoir.

round and take it to him?" But before we had decided, the 'all clear' sounded.

Dorothy Morris

1939

Gas masks were being tried on; then instructions for air raid procedures were given at school. At home we were instructed on how to 'black out' our rooms so not even a chink of light would be visible from outside, by wireless and from the newspapers. Even when I was given my gas mask in its little cardboard box I couldn't believe there would really be a war, with enemy aeroplanes dropping bombs on us! I had seen pictures, (dramatic black and white woodcuts in a large yellow book I had been given by my cousin) of the bombing of Barcelona, and I was very frightened by them.

So when the first sirens sounded soon after war was declared on Sunday morning September 3rd 1939, I expected we would be bombed immediately, or even gassed! My mother's comment was "I *never* thought this would happen in your lifetime!" But my reply was more urgent and more practical: "Michael's gone round to the park without his gas-mask, shall I run

EVACUATION TO WORKINGTON

I don't remember the nature of the arrangements then. Our schools were certainly not included in the evacuation programme, so arrangements were made privately, by my aunts, with contacts they had in Cumberland. It was decided that Michael and I were to travel together to Workington where we would be met and taken to our wartime 'home'. I remember regarding this as a huge adventure at the time, and not feeling too perturbed. I'm not sure what my brother then felt! However, recently he told me his reaction was of excitement, especially at the thought of Euston Station and the 'Lakes Express' which would take the two of us directly to Workington, without having to change trains anywhere. Arrangements must have been made in the days leading up to the declaration of war, for we travelled the following day September 4th.

My brother also retained the impression of excitement from a recent visit to Victoria Station, with our mother to say 'Goodbye' to friends who were returning to Hungary. Although he sensed the prevailing atmosphere of sadness, at ten years old, the steam and the trains and station aura were very thrilling to him. (Neither Mummy or Michael knew in July 1939 that some of our friends from Budapest we would never see again, or know where they were taken to – even though we had seen the swastika stamp on Mummy's passport, as she had had to travel through Germany on her recent return from Hungary).

So, with our gas masks in their cardboard boxes slung across our coats, we climbed aboard the 'Lakeland Express'; a young thirteen year old sister and her small ten year old brother with no conceivable idea of what the immediate or distant future would bring. We hugged and kissed Mummy goodbye and she promised to come and see us soon. We waved to her standing on the platform as the train pulled out of the station. As we sat in the train Michael described to me what he had seen in Princes Park the previous day. "There were soldiers there behind the swings and I saw Arthur Askey and his daughter and I went up to him and told him that war had been declared!", he said. "And you didn't have your gas mask," I commented! It's extraordinary the importance we accorded to the little brown boxes (later to be placed in bright waterproof 6 sided 'envelopes'). We seemed to take them everywhere, though thank God they were never used!

MEMORIES OF MOSLEY IN HYDE PARK

We saw soldiers in uniform on the train, and at all the stations we passed, or stopped at. We both wondered about the fighting. The only mass violence I had ever experienced was on a recent visit to Hyde Park with a friend and her father. Two lots of men seemed to be shouting at each other, and then some of them started fighting the others, and then they all seemed to join in. My friend Wendy and I were hurried away by her father, and we saw policemen on horses riding across the green to the melée. I was very very frightened and I believe I asked Wendy's father if this was a war! "No!" he replied, "it is Mosley's lot I think!"

ARRIVING AT SEATON –'ANOTHER COUNTRY'

At this point I have to say that I have no memory of actually arriving at Workington station and only the vaguest recollection of being taken to the house in Seaton, a small mining village, where we were to live. Perhaps one's memory is very selective. The strange sight of squatting, black-faced men beside the stone walls intrigued me. The ringing sound of what I realised later was the metal on the soles of the clogs of the miners, and others, gave me the impression of arriving in another country altogether. Except I found that we spoke a very similar language, after we had entered a little stone cottage. It was opposite the stone wall and its squatting miners and joined to other similar cottages. There I think we got out of a car with Agnes; who at one time had been our 'Nanny cum mothers help' who introduced us to her brother J and sister in law P. They seemed genuinely pleased to see us.

A WARM WELCOME AT GRAMMAR SCHOOL

At first all seemed well. I remember Mummy visiting us one weekend, and she was received kindly by J and P. Then school started. Michael at first went to the village school, and made very good friends there (one of whom is his close friend today). I went in my Henrietta Barnett uniform to the Grammar School in Workington, it was also a 'Technical College'. There were a few other evacuees, from Grammar Schools in other towns who had come away swiftly like us. The staff and pupils all seemed very kind and it seemed very strange to find myself in a class with boys (and girls) again. It seemed quite a different situation at thirteen and a half, from the mixed classes of Junior School! I soon made friends with many of the girls, and had notes put in my desk by some of the boys!

In the cloakroom one or two girls enjoyed wearing my black velour hat with its bright red hat band, while I tried on their modest little berets! It wasn't long before I was invited to tea by three or four of the girls in my form IVA. I realised that they were miles ahead of me in maths, and cleverer in most of the other subjects.

HELPING AT 'HOME' —BUT PLEASE NO VISITORS!

Of course, Michael and I were aware that we were not receiving the pocket money which had been sent to us. Someone else must have been changing their postal order and forgetting our little share! We had our allotted house tasks, and I became quite adept at dusting the stairs and the skirting boards, tasks which I never resented. Michael and I were now sharing one room which we kept tidy. I don't think we resented this, but although I was allowed to accept my after-school invitations, I was never allowed to ask Mary, Muriel or Joan back. Transport could have been arranged on the after-school bus or service buses from Workington to Seaton and back. I was refused permission for weekend arrangements even if the mother of the friend (sometimes a boy) wrote and asked her permission. I had to stay and do extra house work. However, she could not refuse to allow me to go to Keswick (I believe on the train) to stay with my Auntie Lily and cousins Enid and Ann, who were living there. My Uncle Henry, who did not join them, had rented a beautiful house in its own grounds there.

ABUSE AT 'HOME'

Then there started shouting, and abuse. Food was often withheld and both of us lost weight. My loss was even commented upon by the school nurse! P became pregnant, which put more pressure on pre-school and after-school tasks for us. By this time Michael had passed the scholarship and was coming to school on the bus with his friends who were also successful. This gave another dimension to his life enabling him to suppress the unhappiness we both felt.

I told no-one of the worst experience, either then or in the immediate decade. In fact, not until forty years after the event. Suffice it to say that in my ignorance and innocence I was sexually assaulted by J in the living room, while his pregnant wife was in the bedroom above. It only happened once, but the details and memory of the trauma used to emerge whenever I was not completely absorbed by various interests and activities, and sometimes even during these. Thus when Michael, in despair, suggested we should write and inform our mother of our unhappiness, although at first I insisted we should not worry her, I later gave in and we wrote and told her.

RESCUED BY AUNT LILY FROM KESWICK

By this time the baby had been born and our treatment had worsened. The consequence was that Aunt Lily came over from Keswick, got us to pack our cases, and took Michael to the Heyworth family and his lifelong friend Peter; and me to Mary Kay's home, with her sister and their parents. Aunt Lily had, on hearing from her sister, gone to the headmaster at school and arranged our 'escape'. Michael stayed in Seaton with Peter, his lovely grown-up half-sisters and parents until the end of the war and his schooling. I stayed with the Kays in Workington for over a year, until Mrs Kay's illness. My last year at school, when I gained my Higher School Certificate, I spent with another very kind Workington couple, Mr and Mrs Hesson, whose only son was in the Air Force. So I was rather spoilt there!

I was allowed a very busy social life, the only condition being that whoever took me out had to call for me. There were to be no meetings in the blackout! Also I believe there was a curfew but I don't remember quite what time it was. I was really happy. In addition to dances, visits to the Ice Cream Cafe, Tognarrellis, there were days out at Bassenthwaite and Derwentwater, the Borrowdale Valley, and walks on the lower fells.

MRS CHURCHILL'S AID TO RUSSIA FUND

The war? By this time the Russians were crying out for the allies to launch a 'second front' to engage the German army elsewhere. We had no idea of the extent of the casualties, civilian and military, the USSR was sustaining. My little contribution was to collect for 'Mrs Churchill's Aid to Russia' fund. Dressed in our Girl Guides uniform we carried our tins and smilingly requested donations from anyone who would contribute among the Saturday shoppers. Almost everyone gave generously!

PROGRESS OF WAR

I can't say that we were incredibly aware of the progress of the war. We only knew what the media (not a word used then) of the press, the wireless and the news reel screens revealed to us. We also were aware that last year's VI formers who had joined the Air Force, or the Army or Navy on leaving school (with their Higher School Certificates) were part of it. Only once or twice did the sirens sound while we were in school, necessitating a controlled scramble down to the shelters where we stayed and sang songs until the all clear sounded. Then we all filed out, back to lessons!

SINGING THE WAR SONGS —VERA LYNN

I know the most famous war time singer was Vera Lynn – but she really wasn't the source of my favourite popular music. I don't know now who wrote or sang them but I did love 'That Lovely Weekend' and 'Room 504.' However, of course although I knew all the words of my special favourites, I also joined in 'You are my Sunshine' and 'The White Cliffs of Dover' (but never 'Roll Out the Barrel'!) We often sang while we cycled along the empty country roads in the long summer evenings. One particular evening Mary, Joan and I rode to Cockermouth (I think); and were reprimanded for being late back home by Mrs Kay; although it was nowhere near blackout time when we freewheeled, singing happily, home!

TRAINING TO BE A TEACHER IN SCARBOROUGH

We had made our decisions about our futures and I had been accepted by The City of Leeds Training College to study to be a teacher. This college accepted me although I was just seventeen and a half when I started. (Unlike my first choice, Goldsmiths College, London, which insisted I should be accepted the following year, when I was eighteen). So the following September, after I had been allowed home for the summer holidays (as there had been very little concerted bombing there since the terrible blitz much earlier in the war), I travelled to Scarborough. The college in Leeds was by now a military hospital, so the Training College was housed in hotels in Scarborough. I lived at the 'Dorchester Hotel' with the other girl students who were not in the 'Red Lea Hotel'. The

men were in yet another hotel, and the lecture rooms known as 'Block' in a series of houses on the Filey Road.

EXCITING SCARBOROUGH!

Scarborough was to be an exciting place (for me particularly). At this time its hotels were packed with forces. The RAF in training filled very many as did the army, including soldiers of the 'free' forces. I can remember our hostel tutor, a very respectable spinster, having trouble in trying to warn us against liaisons with the 'free Poles' who weren't quite like the young men we knew! This was before one young lovely student, who liked the Poles, became pregnant!

DANCING AT THE 'ROYAL'

There was dancing at the 'Royal Hotel' almost every night. (I think that I had better explain that dancing meant a boy coming over to a girl and asking her to dance with him). As soon as the band started playing you knew whether it was a 'fun' foxtrot or a romantic waltz (always the last dance) or a 'close together' slow foxtrot. After that dance was over, he either took you back to the group of girls or perhaps asked you for the next dance. The most significant dance was the last waltz. More often than not, your partner for that dance took you home! This could be quite romantic (or sexy) in the blackout! I enjoyed dancing and could 'follow' anyone who could 'lead' (in a terpsichorean sense!). Thus it was very easy to meet soldiers, airmen, an occasional sailor and members of the 'free allied' forces; and later on, Americans most nights at the 'Royal Hotel'!

Having said all this, I did not visit the 'Royal' too frequently as I had a boyfriend in the year above me in college; and until he joined the army on finishing his college course, most of my dancing and socialising was amongst the other students.

1944 - BACK HOME IN LONDON

In the summer of 1944 I was allowed to go home to London. The 'Buzz bombs' had been flying over and exploding, making a weird screaming noise. When the noise stopped, in the silence the bomb exploded!

These 'weapons' were unpredictable and often undetectable so the sirens did not sound and there was no time to run to the shelters. Many people who had had nerves of steel during the blitz could not cope with this 'unknown' danger, and went to stay in the country. Of course I was quite disappointed when I realised I would not be able to go to the theatre, or travel on the tube and enjoy the 'hush hush' Fougasse posters informing me that walls had ears! Also that I would not be able to see my mother or my friends who had stayed in London.

EGERTON ARMS HOTEL IN CHELFORD, CHESHIRE
However I was happy to be going to stay with my Aunt Mimi and Uncle Angelo who ran a pretty little inn in the village of Chelford in Cheshire. It was called the Egerton Arms Hotel. There were three bars (public, private, and a third one for farm workers and others); a lovely little dining room, and six pretty bedrooms, a private lounge and bathroom upstairs. There were also two dogs, Sam the sheepdog and Pim the golden Cocker Spaniel. When I had telephoned them they sounded so pleased to accommodate me, and it was to be a memorable August!

JEEPS BURSTING WITH AMERICANS!
This was to be my first experience of Americans! The roads were full of large lorries (trucks to the Yanks) full of soldiers known as 'GIs'. There were jeeps and cars and other vehicles bursting with men. When they stopped at the little inn, they strode into the public bar requesting a drink. My uncle had already been instructed by their Colonel to use his discretion when serving them. Some were quite happy with one or two drinks to quench their thirst, but others became quite objectionable when refused; even resorting to racist remarks. However, most evenings, Colonel Cook, (who I believe had been in charge of transport at Coca Cola in civilian life) came into the dining room with a very smart uniformed American lady, enjoyed a meal and spent an hour or two chatting with Auntie and Uncle. What I'm sure he didn't tell them, and no one could know then, was that these men who came from their transports to have a drink would soon be going southwards and probably be involved in the D-day attacks, long awaited by France and USSR alike.

SAM THE SHEEPDOG SAVES ME FROM GI ADVANCES
One morning I was taking Sam, the sheepdog cross, for a walk. We went a little way along the main road crowded with troops in trucks, and cut off down a familiar lane. There I took Sam off the lead. As we were walking I had the feeling that I was being followed. I turned round and there was a GI with an orange in his hand (he must have been told that there had been no oranges in England since before the war). He came towards me with his arm outstretched saying "Would you like me to give you an orange?" I was frightened! I was completely alone in the lane, which led to a field beyond a five bar gate. I was well aware of the Yanks' reputation (even worse than the 'free' Poles we had been warned about!). Suddenly Sam sprang forward and started to bark at the man, then I ran as fast as I could and climbed over the gate. By this time Sam had seen the man off and he lolloped towards me. I had never envisaged Sam in the role of protector, he was such a soft loveable creature!

IVY, MY AUNT'S PERSONAL MAID
My aunt had all sorts of people on her staff. Her faithful personal maid Ivy whom she had taken from a 'Home for Orphaned Children' when Ivy was eighteen. Uncle taught her how to bank her wages, and many years later they both were guests of honour at her wedding to a local widower, who had frequented the Egerton Arms, and met her there. (I think Auntie may have sung Ivy's virtues, because she was a very plain girl, but she would do anything for either my Aunt or Uncle).

REFUGEE BILLY FROM AUSTRIA
They also employed a young boy who helped in the kitchen. Billy, fifteen, was a refugee from Austria. He and his brother, Bobby, were rescued by a children's charity just before the war. Bobby was now in the Paratroopers, but he came to Chelford on leave and helped his brother. That summer after Bobby had returned from leave, my aunt asked me if I could fix Billy a little holiday in Scarborough for a week, in a small hotel or boarding house, and look after him while he was there. On my return, this I did. Later I met Billy off the train and took him to his holiday

accommodation on the North Cliff in Scarborough. I had promised Auntie that I would see him as often as I could and take him to the parts of Scarborough which were permissible to visit. Much of the beach and front were cordoned off, as was part of the harbour and pier. So one wet evening we went to the cinema. I wasn't to know this was a mistake. We enjoyed the film. I have no memory of its name because the contents of the newsreel proved to be very traumatic for Billy. There they were, hundreds of aircraft flying over Holland with thousands of paratroopers descending from them! "I'm sure Bobby is there," Billy whispered. Inwardly agreeing with him, I said "No, not necessarily." But Billy was right. Bobby was taken Prisoner of War at Arnhem! Of this we were informed some weeks later, but it wasn't until after the Victory in Europe that the brothers were reunited, and later the world was told what a terrible failure 'Arnhem' had been.

MY COLLEGE DAUGHTER HELEN

Some of my fellow students I really related to, but others I avoided, which I suppose is quite normal. I had a college 'daughter' called Helen, who was nearly a year older than I was (as I had been able to start college a year early having already gained my HSC aged seventeen). She was a pleasant girl and had an unbelievably important influence on my life, of which she would never ever be aware!

VE DAY

The war in Europe continued until, at last, in Spring 1945 the allied tanks rolled across the Rhine. Berlin was occupied, the terrible Concentration Camps were revealed, and Hitler committed suicide. Thus we would celebrate what was known as 'VE Day' on May 8th 1945. At that time I was being fairly faithful to the ex-college friend who was now in the army. Helen came into my room and declared that I had to join her, her army friend Harry, and his friend that evening to celebrate victory at last! "You're not staying in on a special night like tonight!" she told me.

The two soldiers were waiting at the side entrance of our 'Dorchester Hotel'. Helen and I hurried down the steps. She pointed to the shorter of the two. "This is

Harry" she said, smiling. Harry greeted me and then pointed to his tall khaki-clad companion. "This is Arnold," he informed me. [Editor's note: Dorothy was to marry Arnold after the war].

It's quite incredible, but I can't remember any detail of that evening! I know it was very enjoyable. I think we all had drinks in a noisy bar where everyone was celebrating. All I know was that I agreed to see him the following evening

SUMMER 1945 WITH ARNOLD IN SCARBOROUGH

And we spent as much time together as we could in those summer months. On the cliffs, in the Italian Gardens, along the 'front' by the sea, and all the pleasant places in wartime Scarborough. We walked and we talked and we danced! We always danced well together. I had never felt so relaxed, but also stimulated and amused, in any one else's company! I can remember eating 'Baked Beans on Toast' (quite a little feast in those days) in a small cafe at the top of a hill (Scarborough is very hilly!). I was quickly reprimanded by Dolly Wood, our hostel tutor, for watching a group of marching soldiers ascend the hill outside my window, and leaning out and waving when I recognised Arnold! "I didn't expect a well brought up young lady like you Miss Green, would be waving from the window to a soldier!" she said. (I expect it would have been all right if he'd been an officer and not a private!)

Two days later, Arnold attended an officer selection board and was offered a commission in the Infantry. This he refused. (We had previously discussed the reasons for replacement of infantry officers!) He decided he would prefer the Royal Corps of Signals, (where he would quite soon become a Corporal and then a Sergeant – probably not approved of by Dolly Wood!). He then would be posted to a signals base in England and then who knows where?

And of course there was V.J. Day in August 1945. Another victory celebration about which I remember no details at all!

Vera Saunders

LIVING IN THE LAND GIRL'S HOSTEL

I was recruited into the Land Girls, in Leighton Buzzard. There was a hostel with forty girls in it. There was a choice - you could go to a private farm, where you would be living-in, or to the hostel, which I was told was a lot of fun. On May 4th 1942 I joined with my sister Eve (Evelyn) but she wasn't so fit and left after six months. We were taken to the farms in gangs each morning and arrived back later, often very dusty from hoeing, potato picking, 'swede bashing', and in need of a bath. There were only four baths and the water soon ran cold. I spent two years in the hostel. At weekends we could go home. A lot of my time was spent at a farm in Hockliffe and I am still in touch with the family who ran it, and still run it now. I chose to take a driving course in the Land Army.

FAMILY LIFE

We had a lovely family life, played games together, all sat down to dinner together. At the beginning of the war, we lived in Manor Road and Dad worked on the railway. I had three sisters, two brothers. Dad used to listen to the radio on a Cat's Whisker one with headphones. Our curtains showed where they had been burned by acid from the accumulator used for power.

BROTHERS JOINED THE FORCES

My brothers joined the forces - Jack was in the Army, Alan volunteered for the Royal Air Force. He went all over the place, and used to get lifts to come home. On one occasion he had a lift and when he got out, he left his bag of washing in the car. The driver went back to his RAF station and when Alan collected it, the driver's mother had done all the washing!

ALAN COMMEMORATED AT RUNNYMEDE

On the night of 17th/18th January 1943 Alan was on a mission as a Mid-Upper Gunner when he and his crew were posted missing. I never really knew what happened. He is commemorated at the Runnymede Memorial, and in the village. Mother had died the previous October and Eve was looking after my Dad, and my grandparents were at home. Later, we went to Runnymede to see the Queen Mother at the opening and dedication of the Memorial.

CHEDDINGTON SHOPS

In the village Mr Pond sold grocery and all sorts of things. Miss Clarke also sold grocery and sweets. Others called her shop "Tappy May's". The Howletts had a shop with a pump for paraffin and hardware on sale. The Post Office had been just beyond the Slipe in the first of the two Victorian houses but was now opposite the old Chapel. A couple of butchers served the village, Gregory's from Long Marston and Grace from Leighton Buzzard. Janes from Edlesborough came over with shoes and would mend them, too. They are still in business as an electrical shop, as the third or fourth generation. Milk you had from Mr Sayell, or from Will Harrowell, who owned some houses in New Street. There were dances and whist drives, in the tin hut (Church Room) in Station Road, now the Scout Hut.

THE FOG COTTAGES

Down by the station, opposite the wall by the railway lines there were railway cottages known as the fog cottages. When the fog came, down, the signallers were called out to put detonators on the lines as warnings. Since my Dad worked for the railway, we could get a privilege ticket and go into Aylesbury on the local train. Otherwise with a bicycle we went to Leighton Buzzard. We used to cycle all over the place.

Land Army Girls, from left: Sally Townsend (Bedford), Peggy Peter (London), Kath Clarke (Bedford), Vera Saunders (Cheddington), Mary Godfrey (Luton)

Alan Saunders (centre) and colleagues 30th November, 1942

Eileen Gell

LIFE ON THE FARM

I come from a farming family. My mother was born on a farm in Melbourne, Australia. When I could, I joined the Land Army and after working in Devon and Hertfordshire, I was sent here to Cheddington where I was made most welcome by all.

I worked on a farm with a beautiful herd of Jersey cattle. It was a busy life with long hours and we had to work until we finished. We were taken by trucks early in the morning by the brother of the boss, who was a large jolly man who helped us milk in the morning. He was in charge of the outside work, the arable part of the farm. Milking was twice a day and we were allowed a pint of milk at each milking, some we made into butter.

The whole farm and cattle were kept in pristine condition. We even washed the cows' tails. I remember the late Lord Rosebery would bring guests round to see the afternoon milking.

The boss would help with the morning milking and one day he asked if I would like to go to The Ovaltine Farm where they kept a lovely herd of Jersey cattle. It was called The Ovaltine Village and it was beautifully set out. He wanted to buy some small cattle for exporting to South America and they went with some of ours and were shipped from Southampton.

My main job was to look after the small calves and we had a bull that was passed by The Jersey Society. I had to train it to walk on a halter which it did not appreciate at first. One day I was climbing over his pen instead of opening the door and he came behind me and help me over a lot quicker than I expected!

One day there was a bit of horseplay. I was bundled into a wheelbarrow and rushed around the farmyard at great speed just as the boss was bringing round visitors. He remarked to his guests that they work very hard so I expect they can let their hair down sometimes. He never mentioned it again.

He was a good employer and never interfered on the farm. The herd was left to the herdsmen and the outside work to his brother. We had three prisoners of war come and help on the farm, two of them with the cattle. One day we arrived and there was a trail of cream from the dairy to their flat which was on top of the dairy. A lock was then put on the dairy door.

LEISURE TIME

Two of the younger men used to take the prisoners of war to local dances even though they were meant to stop on the farm. Some evenings they would go out rabbit shooting and one evening they shot a fox. We had a very irate gamekeeper come from the estate to the farm the next morning.

On Monday nights we would go to Mentmore village hall where the vicar ran country dancing classes. We also cycled to Leighton Buzzard to the cinema and left our bikes in the alley there with no need to chain or lock them. The Harvest Festivals were much looked forward to and the produce was auctioned off the next day at the village hall now the scout hut with the things on ration making very inflated prices.

VJ DAY

I can't remember VE Day but I remember VJ Day. We were all invited to a get together at The Stag at Mentmore and one of our local farmers did his party piece by singing 'I will take you home again Kathleen.' One of the herdsmen sang 'Oh to be a farmer's boy.' I was volunteered and stood on a table to sing a duet with an airman. We sang "I will give you the keys of heaven".

I remember being in a cottage and the door suddenly opened and the son who had been serving in the Far East arrived home unannounced. He put his kit bag in the corner by the door and completely broke down. I crept quietly away.

Although in many ways there was some very sad times having been in quite a lot of the bombing where I lived in London and elsewhere. We heard nothing of the war in Cheddington after I came here, only the sirens in the distance at Tring. It was a lovely life and I would not have missed it for the world.

Norman Pollard

BORN IN MANOR ROAD

I was born at 5 Manor Road and I was four when the war started. Panic set in throughout the village.

In those days I used to spend the day by myself, left home at half past eight and got home at six o' clock. When I started school my first teacher was Winnie Alderman, my headmaster was Frank Sydney Jeffery.

I can remember the aerodrome and the Italians and then Germans coming later and then the Land Girls.

HARVESTING ON MY BIRTHDAYS

I had my birthday when we were shocking [grouping corn sheaves to stand up close together, Ed.] in the fields. There were no combine harvesters in those days. We were relying on binders and horse drawn, and binders drawn by a tractor. The binder cut the corn like a combine. It was four feet wide and it had a blade that went backwards and forwards. The straw fell down onto a rotating canvas and then it got picked up by two more canvasses running parallel and the straw went in between them. It was collected on the far side of the binder. When the bundle was 12-15 inches in diameter it was tied in a bundle and got knocked out and lay on the ground. Then the Land Army girls would come along, one sheaf under each arm and laid them to make a shock, there were about eight sheaves in a shock. One day it was my birthday and we were shocking and this Land Army girl remembered and gave me a bag of sweets in Windmill Field.

On my ninth birthday I was working for Harrowell. His farm was under the railway bridge between Cheddington and Cooks Wharf, beyond Seabrook Farm. We took German prisoners of war to get the hay in at the fields the Aylesbury side of Puttenham, along the old cattle drive to Aylesbury market. The Germans were quite reasonable guys and they were based in the Camp at Wing, they used to be delivered to farms on lorries. One of the Germans asked me how old I was and I said "Nine" and he said "Nein"!

I heard about the first atomic bomb dropping in Japan from my father at home. Later we discussed it at work in the fields, probably when we were having a cup of tea.

BOMBING LUTON

When they bombed Luton during the war I was down by the canal. We sat down between the road bridge and the iron bridge and we was fishing between there. I was with my brother. We was watching the bombers and the RAF fighters (Spitfires and Hurricanes) flying round the sky and we heard bangs. You couldn't help but hear the noise from the aircraft. Then my father, who was on a day's holiday, came down on his bike and first dragged us under a hedge and then, when it had quietened, he made us walk on the towpath under the bridge. And then we walked home. As the bombers were going to Luton, the fighters were following them. We thought the bombers were aiming for Vauxhalls , that was the story that weekend.

LONG MARSTON AND MENTMORE HIT

A bomb dropped on the school at Long Marston and killed one of the teachers, she had just sent the school kids home. Vera Saunders was a Land Army girl and Kathleen her sister was a teacher at Long Marston school.

Two bombs went off up Mentmore Road during the night. I can remember my father getting us all downstairs and under the dining table (with the old fashioned scrub top).

THE SCHOOL

The Schoolteacher was Winnie Alderman. We all had a little gas mask in a tin with a piece of string coming out the end and it went round your neck. She used to give us, in the classroom, practices to get the gas mask on and off. They reckoned we would only have seconds to put it on if gas was dropped. They took us for fire practice with our gas masks on. We used to have to get under this hedge between the allotments and Frank Williams' orchard.

There were three classrooms, infants, middle and senior. We used to have Sports Day, high jumping and running. There was a bowling green in Bowling Green Meadow with an iron fence round it (it used to belong to Lord Rosebery but Ned Bishop farmed it). We used to hold Sports Days in that or on The Green.

In the main classroom where the clock strikes, all up by the side of the clock cupboards there was grey blankets and big tins of food and powdered drink. We never did know what was in them. They just disappeared as did the blankets.

THE EVACUEES

The evacuees came one evening and I think it was Mrs Stoddart who lived down the Manor, she went round asking people to take in evacuees. I can remember my mum and dad went down to the school and they came back with two evacuees, Sidney and Bob Bird. They had an elder sister and younger brother and they went down the Manor. They didn't last too long, the younger one went back to his mother, then Bob Bird went down to the Manor and Sidney stayed with us for ages. Sidney Bird came to see me long after the war.

In all honesty I think we used to bully them a bit. We used to call them the 'Cor blimeys.' The evacuees started mixing with the local boys and we had two gangs - the village boys and the station boys, and we were blood enemies. We used to go down the recreation ground and dig up chalk and throw it at each other. We used to get cut heads and faces, nothing serious, just youngsters throwing stuff. It used to give us something to do.

THE END OF THE WAR

I don't remember a great deal about the end of the war. I can't remember whether my memory is of the end of the war in Europe or the end of the war in Japan, but I went down The Green in the morning on my bike and there was a barrel organ and I can't remember if it was Sammy Chandler turning the handle.

Maurice Horn

HEARING CHAMBERLAIN'S ANNOUNCEMENT

I was 13 in August as the war started in September. All my wartime years I was in my teens. On my birthday I thought war was definitely coming.

My first memory of war was the declaration of war by Mr Chamberlain on September 3rd. We'd just had a brand new wireless, I remember, a Cossor. It was about two feet six inches wide by two feet tall. It was the first electric wireless that my parents had. I always remember a lot of the lads that were military age, gathered at the bottom of our garden on the High Street to hear Chamberlain speaking. At the end of the broadcast they went away looking very despondent. Our house was where the new school is now. There was a row of eight little cottages there.

THE EVACUEES ARRIVE

In the afternoon of the day war was declared, we watched the arrival of two coachloads of evacuees from the East End of London at Cheddington School. Their ages ranged from five years old to twelve years old. The billeting officers, mostly from the local Women's Institute, were waiting to take them to their new homes.

GERMANS DROP BOMBS ON MENTMORE SPINNEYS

I s'pose my next memory is the Germans dropping a stick of bombs along Mentmore Spinneys about May 1940, a Saturday night, before they started bombing London properly. They kept the road shut on the Sunday and they didn't reopen the road till Monday. As soon as it was open all us boys went along Mentmore Road on our bikes to see where the bombs had landed. The craters were 20 feet deep at least. We picked up some of the shrapnel .

AUXILIARY FIRE SERVICE

When I was 16 I joined the Auxiliary Fire Service, which every village had. There were altogether 16 of us and we went on duty every eighth night from 10pm to 6am, just in case they dropped incendiaries. Our captain was Sammy Chandler, he lived in New Street and then Manor Road. The vice-captain was Freddie Bartholomew, he lived at the top end of New Street. As far as I remember we only ever had three fires to deal with, one was on Mr Bishop's field, a hayrick and one a chimney fire in Horton. I gather they put the hose down the top of the chimney, I was at work at the time. With the hayrick fire luckily there was a pond in the field and we got that fire out quite easily.

We used to stand out the High Street watching the Germans bomb London because you could see the glow of fire all along the Chiltern Hills.

The third fire we had was our own fireman's hut. We had a stove in there with a narrow nine inch diameter chimney stack which went through the roof. We were in the High Street watching fires over London, a bad night for London in December 1940, and the two firemen on duty, they came down and joined in the crowd who were watching fires all over London, when all of a sudden someone turned round and said "Chaps your chimney's on fire," and the two firemen scurried off and put some wet sacks down the top of the chimney!

We used to do exercises every Sunday morning fitting the hosepipes onto the hydrants. We must have looked like the Keystone Kops!

Of course as far as I can remember in addition to us firemen being on duty there was four Home Guard, one ARP warden and two special constables who used to go round shouting "Put that light out!"

The ARP warden lived in the bottom cottage of Mason's yard. He used to get the warning about imminent air raids by telephone, before the sirens went off.

THE RAF AND THEN THE AMERICANS ARRIVE

During the war there was numerous plane crashes in this area which used to get us boys racing off on our bicycles to where it had taken place.

The biggest memory of all was when the RAF and Americans took the airfield over at Long Marston.

Especially when the Americans came, the size of the Flying Fortresses and Liberator bombers, they were all four engines and we had never seen anything that big before. On Sunday afternoon us boys used to go up to the Linces and see the Fortresses practising and taking off and landing.

The American airmen were very friendly, pretty free with their cigarette packets. They used to give us loads of cigarettes and sweets. The cigarettes were Chesterfields, Lucky Strikes and the worst ones were Camel, they were rotten. Of course the Americans were very friendly, especially with the girls. In fact we had three girls married to Americans, Jean Foxon, Peggy Cleaver and my cousin Olive Wesley married Bob Smith from Louisville. After the war they went out to America as GI brides. Sadly Olive was only in America 12 months when she caught consumption (TB) and died. Of course the Americans spun the girls such tales and the girls saw films and thought they were going out to mansions.

The RAF were quite a good bunch of blokes. They flew Wellington twin engined bombers. They came at the end of 1941 and the Americans took over in 1942.

One Sunday morning at 10am we heard this terrific noise of aircraft going over. We all rushed out to look and there were all these aircraft pulling huge gliders and about four or five hours later we saw these planes coming back with no gliders and then on the six o' clock news we heard that the gliders had landed in Arnhem. The Germans first used gliders early in the war. The gliders carried about 50 men in them. There would have been no engine noise and the men were dropped off. But a huge number crash-landed and killed all the men inside.

D-DAY BOMBINGS
Another memory was when I was on fire duty on 5th June 1944. A procession of aircraft kept going over during the night and when we came off duty at 6am in the morning the Lancasters were flying out very low because the Americans were going out over the top of them to carry out bombing the German fortifications along the Normandy coast. We knew there was something big going on (D-Day was on 6th June) and in

the morning on the news we heard that the Allied forces had begun landing in France.

STARTING WORK
I finished school at 14 and I went to work in Aylesbury at the Agro electrical factory near the Royal Bucks Hospital. It had just been converted over to making spare parts for aircraft. I was only there for about seven or eight months, I didn't like it at all. I came back then and became a milkman. I worked for Harrowell on Seabrook Farm, one of the happiest jobs I ever had. I used to drive a horse and cart with the milk. The horse got to know every stop, you didn't have to tell them. I delivered round Cheddington, Ivinghoe and Pitstone. It was mostly loose milk, we used to have several churns holding 16 pints and you measured it out with a jug with a long handle. It measured one pint and the customers held the jug to be poured in at the door. It was only towards the end of the war that the bottled milk came in. We used to deliver milk in the morning and wash the bottles, with a special powder and brush, in the afternoon. Towards the end it was all bottles. The dairy was part of Seabrook Farm. I worked in the dairy but never milked a cow!

CALLED UP!
After being a milkman I was called up into the Army in December 1944. It was a very big shock! I was a conscript. I was still doing basic training in Bury St. Edmunds when the war finished on May 8th.

When the Japanese war finished I was in the Military Hospital at Aldershot and from there I was discharged from the Army with chronic bronchitis.

By the time I came home in the November, all the planes had gone from the airfield. When I come home I went gardening for the Earl of Rosebery at Mentmore Towers, that's where I met my wife.

Eve Sharp, nee Bishop

BORN INTO A FARMING FAMILY

I was born in the middle cottage the other side of the railway towards Horton. It was then in Cheddington Parish.

One year later we moved into a council house in Manor Road where we stayed until I was eighteen years old. Before and during the Second World War the farms around Mentmore were owned by Lord Rosebery. My grandfather, Ned Bishop, had come to Cheddington as a tenant farmer at Town Farm after one of his brothers, Richard, took over the family farm at College Green, Aston Clinton. The two brothers had been farming with their father but there was only room for one to take over the farm. My grandfather, Ned, had eight children: five boys and three girls. My father Charles (Charlie) was the second youngest boy. Town Farm was a mixed farm of about 360 acres. It included South End Hill, a field across the other side of the canal and the field where Keeper's Cottage, (now called Falcon House) stands. The gamekeeper to Lord Rosebery lived there. The farmhouse was large and the kitchen floor was stone on earth. When a pig was killed it was salted and hung to season in the kitchen. The abattoir, run by Mr. Charlie Jellis and his father, was at Old Farm in Pitstone.

In front of the kitchen, in the yard, was a trough where the bull was brought to drink, its nose ring attached to the end of a pole. Next to the kitchen was the dairy. Bert Wesley was Grandad's cowman. The dairy herd was of about thirty cows. The family had their own milk from the cows but the rest was collected at the gate by the Milk Marketing Board. There was no cream or butter at home as it would have spoiled the quality of the milk. The milking parlour, at Town Farm, backed onto the road. We used to drive the cows down the road to the Swan Orchard, near the Old Swan public house then on to Keeper's Meadow. The male calves were fattened for Tring livestock market. A lot of bargaining and 'wheeling and dealing' went on in the Robin Hood public house in Tring, on market days. There was a flock of 100 sheep – Hampshire Downs, and about six sows for breeding from the Elsage Farm boar. A few chickens were also kept. The crops grown were wheat, barley, oats, swedes, turnips plus mangel-wurzels for cattle feed. The corn was cut with a binder and there were no chemicals so there were as many thistles as corn stalks. I remember there being four men working on the farm. One, 'Punch' Chandler, who looked after the horses, Boxer and Dolly, was from Long Marston. We also had a Land Girl, I think from Wing, working on the farm. The Land Girls lived in a hostel in Wing and came down each day. We were lucky having the farm as we had plenty of milk and eggs and, like most other people, we grew our own vegetables. At Manor Road we had very long gardens. We lived at number 4 Manor Road and later, when Sunnybank was built, one of our apple trees was in the garden of the fourth house along. We had a black lead range which had to be lit each morning before we could have a hot drink. My father brought home wood from the farm. My father kept about six hives of bees as a hobby and I remember him in his bowler hat covered by a net tied under his chin and with string tying up his trouser bottoms and sleeves. Yet still he got stung! We had pet rabbits in the garden which 'would disappear', as would the older chickens.

FOOD AND PRODUCE

There were three allotments in the village: one where the present village hall stands, one behind what is now Sunnybank, and one opposite where the tennis courts are now, which was half owned by Lord Rosebery, and half by the Parish Council. Sid Harrowell sold milk door-to-door from his pony and cart. He and his brother Will had Seabrook Farm, under the railway, and took the cows over the swing bridge to the field. There were three General Stores in the village: Mason's on the High Street, Mr Pond on The Green and Miss May Clark, known as 'Tappy May' for her habit of tapping the scales in her favour, towards Barkham Close. Besides the usual groceries there was paraffin and coal for sale. There was a coal merchant near the station, in a siding by the branch line to Aylesbury. A baker came round every other day, with a handcart, from Mr Stallard's bakery in Pitstone although there was a baker by Christmas Cottage on The Green. A grocer came from Leighton Buzzard on Mondays to take orders for delivery Thursday or Friday. Mr Gregory, the butcher, came from Long

Marston on Mondays to take orders for delivery on Wednesday and Friday.

THE AIRFIELD

On Cheddington Airfield, first the RAF and later the Americans, were based. One day we saw some off-duty RAF men walking on the rough piece of ground where Sunnybank is now. My mother held up the teapot to them and four came for tea and cake. They said how it made them feel homesick.

THE OLD SWAN

My friend's parents, Mr and Mrs Bert Castle, kept The Old Swan. They had five children. Two older sons were in the Navy and two younger sons were at school. My friend, Phyllis, was the only girl. The Yanks often came in to The Swan. They were very generous and gave us sweets and chewing gum.

STRETCHING THE RATIONS FOR VISITORS

My mother's family were from Sutton in Surrey. The three sisters and their families used to visit here. Because we were in the country they didn't understand that we were also rationed. The cousins worked in a high class clothing shop and were looking for clothing coupons. My mother exchanged coupons for their old clothes which she would carefully unpick and remake into clothes for us, e.g. a 'swagger' coat used a lot of material so she could make more than one item from it. In the afternoons she used to go up to The Manor to join a group, I think, to sort clothes.

MY FATHER AND THE ROC

My father was in the ROC and on duty Saturday and Sunday nights on West Hill, so he had no sleep until Monday. Monday evenings there was a slide show in the school for the ROC to help them identify British and German planes. They were shown slides of the planes taken from different angles. If an enemy plane was spotted they had to phone through to the next post to alert them. I think 'Love Two' was the code name of their base. One old boy was on duty when the phone rang with a warning and asked for an estimate of the height of the aircraft. He replied that, as he couldn't see them they must be above the stars. When

my father was on duty we all slept in the same bed and once heard a bomb drop near by. A bomb fell on Long Marston School just an hour after school finished, and a teacher was killed.

OUR EVACUEE

We had an evacuee living with us. The school brought in a group, by train, to Cheddington station and they walked from there to the school. They were just 'dished out'. It was based on your accommodation and the size of your family. They were standing in a group and someone would grab them by the collar and 'give' them to someone. Luckily our boy, John Jerack, loved farming and he was treated like one of the family. When he was thirteen he left to return home. He didn't want to go and although he had been with us for quite a while, his family had never visited him. My mother could never understand why we didn't hear from him again. Did he run away?

George Bishop, Eve's uncle

John Meacham

COUSIN SALUTED NEVILLE CHAMBERLAIN

I was 10 at the beginning of the war and on Sunday 3rd September 1939, I was with my mother and brother and cousin. My cousin, who was in his Scout uniform, saluted Neville Chamberlain during his broadcast.

THE EVACUEES

Soon after, evacuees were billeted round the village, although some went back during the so called phoney war.

The evacuees took over the Church Room (now the Scout Hut) as a school under Mr Spary, a teacher from London, but he wasn't there for long.

LIGHT PLANE IN ORCHARD

Shortly after a light plane came down by the orchard by Church path flown by a Fleet Air arm (naval) pilot. He was tangled in the trees and was cut down by Lal Wesley and was bandaged by women of the village who had trained in first aid. Two or three years later the pilot came back to the village to thank the First Aiders.

HOME GUARD AND OBSERVER CORPS AND BLACKOUT

Men of the village were in the Home Guard and Air Raid Wardens and the Observer Corps had an observation place on top of the Westend Linces.

The blackout was well observed but caused some difficulties. It was a bit chancy getting about with no lights. You can imagine people observing at the Linces changing guard and having to get home in the dark . And they still had their day job to go to.

DEATHS OF JOHN SHAND KYDD AND LONG MARSTON HEADMISTRESS

I remember the death of John Shand Kydd when his plane crashed in Horton. I also remember when the Headmistress at Long Marston School was killed when it was hit by a direct hit.

RUSSIAN OFFICERS IN THE GOODS YARD

I recall when high ranking Russian Officers were in uniform staying in train carriages in Cheddington goods yard, there were about six to ten officers there. The rumour was that they were a delegation coming to see Winston Churchill, but that is only speculation, I don't know if that is correct.

AMERICANS LEAVE THE AERODROME

Later when the Americans were leaving the aerodrome, they were all lined up five abreast waiting for the trains, from the station to the Rosebery Arms.

All in all Cheddington was a good friendly place despite the rationing etc.

Christine Steed

Christine is Lionel (Len) Steed's mother. She came to live in England after the war.

MY FAMILY FLEES GERMANY

I was born in Ostfriesland, Germany in 1925, but my family moved to Hamburg when my father worked on a shipping line in Hamburg. Sadly my father died in 1933 aged only 26.

In 1937 my mother remarried, to Walter Seidler, and they had a child called Walter – my half brother. I had two sisters and one little brother and we lived in a beautiful flat. One day we were all playing in the sandpit outside and suddenly the sirens went. "What's that?" we said, and someone said war had started, so we all went quickly upstairs to our flat.

My step-father was born in Morasko, a little village near Poznan in Poland (although he was German), he was still quite young and had studied engineering. He was from a very rich family. My step-father had a sister and she married a rich man and my brother had lived with them in Poland in a mansion.

My step-father's brother in law (he owned a bank and four different businesses) told us to pack immediately and go and live in Poland. A big transporter arrived and took all the beautiful furniture, including the white piano, and it was all transported by rail to the mansion.

ARRIVING AT THE POLISH MANSION

When we arrived at the mansion it had beautiful gardens. It was situated next to a castle. In the castle there were all sorts of people who had nowhere to live and had just moved in.

We were quite happy in our house. We had servants and gardeners and endless, endless vegetables and flowers and we collected huge bowls of raspberries from the gardens. We had plenty of money and the servants were paid well, and my mother treated them well. If we had sweets then they had sweets. Everything was made for us, hats, shoes and dresses.

We would sit in our favourite restaurant, The Arcadia, with our new outfits on. We had a fantastic life.

EXPLOSION KILLS CHILDREN

I'm in my lounge, my brother was 5 or 6, suddenly I heard a most terrible explosion. The Germans had made a mound of earth and potatoes were kept there for the following year. The Germans left something there that exploded and four little Polish boys died, they were all Walter's friends.

GENERALS VISITED US

Generals and high-up officers used to go to our lake and swim. I nearly drowned there several times. Lots of guests used to stay at the house and I went to the river with a little girl. I could not get out of the current and who should come along but two little airmen on a day out and they laid me down on their boat and took me back to the little girl. We used to have lovely picnics with the soldiers.

WORKING AS A MEDICAL ASSISTANT

Little Walter went to the local school, my sister went to the college. I worked as a medical assistant in various hospitals. I gave injections, assisted in operations and worked in the laboratory. If you wanted to know if a woman was pregnant we would inject a mouse with her urine. Then I would take the mouse, kill it and open her up. If the inside was swollen we knew that the woman was pregnant.

DIPHTHERIA

Unfortunately at the time when diphtheria was rife, I was taking blood from a little girl and I caught diphtheria from her. I was paralysed and blind for eight months. But, as you see, I recovered. My mother came from Poznan to see me and said to an SS Army doctor "How is my daughter?" He answered brusquely "She won't live." But sure enough I did! This was because we had a professor and he invented a pea, and eating this green pea made me better.

I was kept in isolation in just one room. Diphtheria was bad, it was so bad. When each new case arrived at the hospital, a bell rang and the doctors did whatever they could for the patient. I recovered after endless months in hospital.

Clockwise from left: sisters Katerina, Anna, and Christine,
Anna (mother) and a German soldier, share a meal.

Anna and Christine walking with family and
friends in the grounds of the mansion

THE GERMAN OFFICERS QUARTERS IN THE MANSION

The mansion house was a listed building and we lived there between 1940 and 1945 in the downstairs part of the house. It used to be a guest house for the castle next door and Von Tresckow lived there. He was the infantry division chief of staff in the invasion of Poland and was later involved in the attempted murder of Hitler. [The house was requisitioned by German Generals from the front line for rest and recuperation, Ed.] The house had 12 rooms upstairs which were all occupied by officers. Every officer had a bell in their room which rang in the kitchen and the batman would attend to the officer when the bell rang. We had a very big kitchen iron stove with four ovens. The batman came and got their officer the food. Everyone had a chair, there were 40 chairs in the dining room. We would invite ordinary soldiers for a Sunday roast.

We had a fantastic time with the officers and the generals stationed in Poznan, great big parties. They went shooting in the forest. Poland is a lovely country and has lots of forests. All sorts of animals living in the forest were shot and hung on hooks in the outbuildings. I liked all that stuff.

Some days the officers would phone to ask whatever animal they wanted to be prepared for cooking. The servants prepared a feast and then afterwards we would dance with the officers. They were very kind and saved our lives. We were the only people in the village to have a telephone. They said "We will let you know when to go, and when we say 'go' go quickly". [The generals knew in 1942 that the war would be lost, it was planned that a general would ring the house to let the family know when the Russians were coming, Ed] On 25th January, 1945 the phone call came to say that the Russians were advancing. The Russians had a reputation for raping women when they invaded an area.

THE SEVEN SUITCASES

Before we left we had two great big turkeys for dinner at 5pm that evening. My mother packed as much as possible into seven carefully labelled suitcases. We had to leave everything else in the house behind, including some very valuable antiques.

WE LEFT THE MANSION BY HORSE AND CART

We felt terrible when we left the house at 5am the next morning. We didn't go to bed the last night or get undressed. The burgomaster would not take us to the station he said "You are against Hitler." But of course we had pictures of Hitler on the wall – we had to. A little Polish farmer took us from Morasko to Poznan. We travelled by horse and wooden cart to Poznan train station, with the seven suitcases and we stayed for two days at the hotel at the station. Then we left to board a train to Zwickau in Germany. But there was chaos and the German Army officials would let only people board and we had to leave the seven cases standing on the platform.

Infants died on the train and were thrown from the window .

STAYING WITH A FRIEND IN ZWICKAU

When we got to Zwickau we stayed with a friend in his flat. He was a chemist and also an antiques dealer. We had brought four chickens with us from Poznan and we ate one every evening for four days. When we had run out of food we went to get some more food coupons but we were told we could not claim them unless we worked in a munitions factory. As we had no means of getting food and our friend had only a few food coupons, we had to move on.

SIX WEEK JOURNEY TO OSTFRIESLAND

We left for Zwickau station and headed for Ostfriesland to see our family again. The journey took six weeks. We had some money but could not buy much with it, so we were starving. We kept passing farmers on platforms with bread and great big sausages, but the farmers would not share them with us.

THE SEVEN SUITCASES ARRIVED IN ZWICKAU!

Once in Ostfriesland a letter arrived from Zwickau to tell us that the cases had arrived. I was now 19, and I decided to go with my 16 year old sister, Anne, to return to Zwickau to pick up the cases. On our journey back, which took six weeks, we tried to get into Hamburg, Berlin and Hanover, but each time we were told that the way was blocked because the towns were still being bombed. When we finally got to Zwickau we were exhausted and hungry and so we stayed in our friend's flat again. All we could hear was thousands of bombers going overhead to bomb Dresden.

BOMBING RAID ON LEIPZIG

We then returned to Ostfriesland with the seven suitcases by train. On the way we had to get off the train and walk through Leipzig with the suitcases. A bombing raid on Leipzig had just stopped and houses were on fire and falling down around us. Lots of people helped us to carry the cases.

HOME BY MIDNIGHT TAXI TO LEER!

Eventually we arrived back home in Leer, Ostfriesland at 1.30am with the seven suitcases. Luckily we managed to get a taxi home – a miracle with all those suitcases. At the sight of us my mother almost fainted with shock, she thought that she was never going to see us again!

INVASION BY CANADIANS AND BRITISH

In Ostfriesland there was the first invasion of the Canadians and British as the Allied Forces came in. The Canadians came in tanks but got very stuck in the meadows. Every house had a white sheet outside to let the soldiers know that they would not resist the Allies. The Canadians used to have drinks with us, but one of our family always had to drink the liqueur first in case we were trying to poison them.

One time two Canadian brothers came to look after my sister, brother and me. They stayed all night but they didn't try anything. In contrast one night a drunken English official came and banged on the door and pushed a pistol in my chest and demanded to sleep with me. Luckily by some miracle the official's young batman managed to stop him from doing this. The same official went to the next house and raped a woman and she ended up with a baby because of it.

THE POLES ARRIVE

The first division of the Poles also arrived in Ostfriesland and the Poles hated the Germans so we had to be really careful. Luckily our family was OK because my step-dad knew some of the Polish soldiers from when we lived in Poland and we had always been very kind to them.

GERMAN SOLDIERS REPAIR THE CANAL BRIDGES

Where we lived there were lots of canals with tiny bridges, they were made of planks, used to step over the canal as there were houses on each side. The bridges had all been destroyed by explosives laid by German soldiers. This made it more difficult to cross so we built makeshift planks. When the war ended the German soldiers became prisoners of the British and Canadians and they were forced to rebuild the bridges.

Ken Webb

TRAINING BY POLICE

At the beginning of the war I was 15 and the police messaging service came to my house and I was told to report to Leighton Buzzard Police Station. I went on my bike and I was given armband, gas mask, and a blue steel helmet which had 'Police' written on the front. I went to lectures at the Police Station. One night, when I was there, some fire bombs were dropped on Leighton Buzzard. I was told to lie on the floor for a few minutes to see what was happening. When I went to the door afterwards there was a fire bomb on the doorstep and we had to go out the other way and put sandbags round it.

HEATH AND REACH BOMBED

I started to go out with the police. One night I was on duty, bombs were dropped on Heath and Reach. There were four. The biggest one was in Sylvester Street. Some of the ceilings came down in the houses and greenhouses were wrecked. A fire bomb landed in Thomas Street and Mavis Williams was running down the street to her sisters to see if her children were all right and another fire bomb fell on her shoulder. She was killed instantly. She was only 17. A million and one chance of that happening.

I carried on going out with the police in my spare time and worked at RENE experimental works in Grovebury Road. I can remember when I was on duty one day and a Dornier 217 flew over the roof tops and went up the A5 and dropped bombs by The Fox and Hounds pub.

CALLED UP AND POSTED TO GERMANY

I was called up when I was 20 and I went to Yatesbury, Wiltshire, for my training. I was then posted to Carlisle for a few weeks and then went to Elvington near York. It was a Halifax bomber station. After a few weeks there, I was posted to Great Sampford police school and then sent to Germany when the war was nearly over. I went all over Germany. I went to Cuxhaven near the Baltic Coast When we got there the sea was all froze over.

I then went to Hamburg on the vice squad and after that I was on escort duty taking prisoners across Germany. I then went to Ruhr area where most of the big industries were. I went on to Essen. It was nearly all bombed. I can remember the Krupps factory there. Not a lot left of that. I then went to Wuppertal which had the world's first hanging railway.

NEW HITLER YOUTH 'PRODUCTION'

Then we went to Bad Meinburg. There was a castle there and we slept in the hospital which was as modern as one today. Young women were having children there and they were given a badge for each child they had. The children were taken away from their mothers to be the new Hitler Youth. The young women had been specially picked and had to go through strict medicals. The men were specially picked, some SS men, the elite of the German army. I was there for six weeks and then picked up by S Investigation Branch. I went to Wahn near Cologne. I was there for a few weeks and then I was expected to go to Japan but the Americans had dropped the atomic bomb and I did not go.

MARRIED ON LEAVE

I did not get any leave until October 1946. The weekend I came home it was Ethel's birthday and we got married. She had done all the arrangements while I was away. We got married in Heath and Reach Church and then we went to St Leonard's, Hastings for our honeymoon. I was on leave only for 10 days and then went back to Germany. Ethel came up to London to see me go.

COLOGNE THEN BACK TO LEIGHTON BUZZARD

I was posted back to Cologne and then after a week I was told I had been posted back to England to Leighton Buzzard. I thought he was pulling my leg but it was true. I went to Oxenden House headquarters for radar work and went on a bike backwards and forwards for duty. After a few weeks there I went to a golf course near Blackpool. I handed all my equipment in and was given a demob suit and a trilby.

Ken Webb (on right) with colleagues

Devasted Cologne Cathedral. Reports vary on how many times the Cathedral was hit by aerial bombs during the Second World War. Internet sources state between 14 and 70 times.

Bombed out Krupps works at Essen. Krupps suffered heavy bombing between 2nd and 6th March 1943. Reconnaissance photographs indicate 53 buildings were hit by bombs during this time.

A collapsed Rhine bridge at Cologne. Is this the Cathedral bridge?

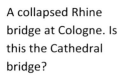

Jane Cutler

Doris (Nancy) Kirke

Frederick Brown

PARENTS MET IN LEIGHTON BUZZARD

I was born during the war in July 1944. My parents, Doris (Nancy) Kirke and Frederick Brown, were married in September 1943 at St Johns Church in Boxmoor. My father had secured a 48-hour pass from the RAF. They met in late 1942 in Leighton Buzzard. My mother was a Corporal in the WAAF, and my father, also a Corporal, was in the RAF and stationed at the Marley Tiles site. They spent the evening of their wedding day on an outing to London where they enjoyed a meal and saw a West End play. They then caught the last train back to Boxmoor, to spend the night at my mother's home in Sebright Road.

FATHER TRAINED AS A GUNNER

Prior to meeting my mother, my father had volunteered for Aircrew and, at the time of the wedding, he had just successfully completed an Air Gunner's course at RAF Station Morpeth and now had his Sergeant's stripes. He was later assigned to 514 Squadron of Bomber Command stationed at Waterbeach.

BAILED OUT OVER BELGIUM

On 11th May 1944 the Lancaster, in which my father was a mid upper gunner, was shot down by the Germans and caught fire over Rixensart in Belgium. He bailed out by parachute (thus becoming eligible for membership of The Caterpillar Club). After being hidden by the Underground movement in Belgium, he was eventually caught after a tip-off to the Gestapo and, after a period of interrogation, imprisoned in Stalag Luft VII.

ANXIOUS TIME FOR MY MOTHER

In the meantime, my mother, now heavily pregnant, was informed by telegram that her husband was missing. There followed a very anxious time for her. For 13 weeks she thought that Fred had been killed. Then she heard that one of the Lancaster's crew had turned up and there was hope that my father was still alive. During this period I made my arrival in July at West Herts Hospital, Hemel Hempstead.

Towards the end of the war on 8th February, 1945 my father was moved to Stalag IIIA in Luckenwalde about 20 kilometres south of Berlin.

He has written a detailed diary and accounts of the war period in his, as yet unpublished, book "Get Fell In". The following piece is an extract from this book.

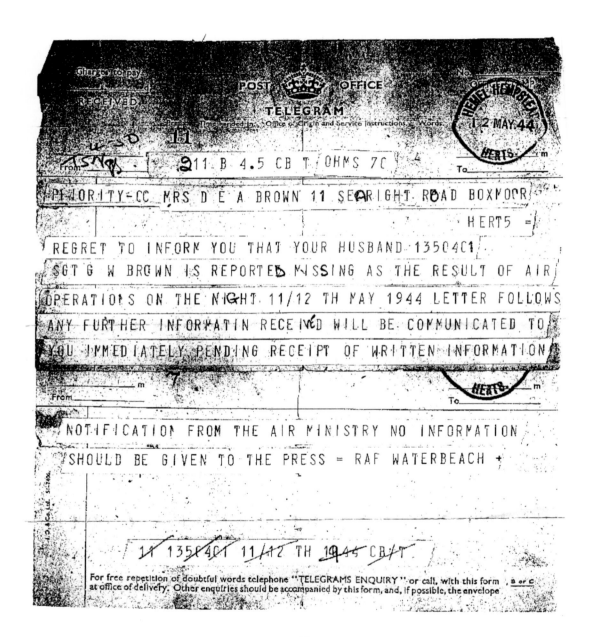

A copy of the telegram, dated 12th May 1944, sent to Mrs D E A Brown informing her that her husband 'G' W Brown was reported missing as a result of air operations on the night 11/12th May 1944.

Frederick Brown

SUNDAY 1ST APRIL 1945, STALAG IIIA

Here my diary stops so its memories from now on. Things don't alter much from day to day. When the weather's fine we feel good, when it's cold and wet we feel miserable. There's no comfort to be had in the barracks, cold barns really. Appels are morning and night, we are counted and recounted, it's easy to slip in and out of the columns to confuse the count.

The guards are becoming slack, and friendly, more friendly by the day. They like we realize the war is coming to an end. We have radio bulletins twice a day, more if there's any important news. Rumours abound, we are to be moved to Bavaria. A group of officers are taken to Luckenwalde station. After four days awaiting a train they return, the railway system is at a standstill. It was rumoured the officers were to be held hostage.

The camp is receiving more POWs everyday. Some civilians too. All nationalities, they are arriving from areas now overrun by the Russian advance. All including the guards are in an awful state. They pass our compound coming from the main gate. They will swap anything for a cigarette. I picked up a good pen knife for two cigarettes, then someone got a wristwatch for just one. They all look so pathetic.

Food issues are low, no bread at all, just one serving of weak soup per day. Our Red Cross parcels are keeping us alive. When an issue of bread was made, it was a loaf between 16 men, hardly a thin slice each.

The sound of the battle could be heard in all directions. Aircraft constantly overhead, Russian aircraft appeared, slow compared with the Allied and German aircraft.

We lived in a constant air of expectancy, German tanks and troops moving toward Berlin, columns passing each day. The camp was passed as though we were a cancer on the landscape.

Stalag IIIA was at bursting point, tens of thousands of POWs, plus Italian civilians. The Russians still went out on working parties, coming back with bundles of wood for sale. They also had another item for sale, strips of white cloth. At first we couldn't see the significance of the cloth, then the penny dropped, these pieces of cloth were surrender flags.

We had hoped the Allies would liberate us, this was becoming unlikely. Each day the canary told us the Russians were getting closer to the camp. We had some Canadians who spoke Russian they told us that the Russian POWs hoped that the Allies would liberate them, they didn't expect to be well treated by their fellow countrymen.

14TH APRIL 1945 HEAVY RAF BOMBING

The night of April the 14th was a Guy Fawkes night. The RAF put on a vivid bombing display, they attacked Potsdam not 10kms away. The ground shook, we watched as the markers fell, in fact it was really too close, some bombs fell close to the camp. Bombs had fallen within the camp in the last month. The next day we heard that hundreds of bombers had been on this raid. Keith Campbell wrote, it was an awe inspiring sight.

SUNDAY 22ND APRIL: GERMANS DESERT CAMP

The previous days, the German Administration had been keeping a low profile, the Russians, we knew were close to Luckenwalde. We were woken by a bod who had gone to the latrine at first light. He came into the barracks shouting,

"The goons have gone, the goons have gone."

As one man, we made a dash for the doors, he was right, not a German to be seen. Not a goon in a tower, not a goon in the camp.

We were delirious in our joy. What would happen now?

THE PRISONERS TAKE OVER RUNNING THE CAMP

The senior officers had already planned for this moment. Within a short time the gates and offices were manned by German and Russian speaking RAF men.

About 7 or 8am, we heard the sound of gunfire in Luckenwalde and Jutterbug. Then the Russian front line tanks came into sight. One tank came into the camp, the crew waving, then it proceeded to crush the barbed wire around the compounds. We waved and cheered. We watched the front line troops go through, motorbikes and sidecars, all sorts of odd transport, no back-up stores, these chaps lived off the land.

They offered rifles, made signs we should go with them, no one did. In retrospect I wish I had been in at the fall of Berlin. Surely an historic event to be remembered. Only two or three nights previously, two RAF bods had been shot trying to escape, if only they had waited. The SBO (Senior British Officer) issued an order: "No one to leave camp. This for our own safety."

MONDAY 23RD APRIL: FORAGING FOR FOOD
We began to settle down, the euphoria passed. The SBO had taken over, the Orderly Room organised. Forage parties were out, searching for food, fuel anything that would be of use. A list of tradesmen were called for. I registered as a baker. Well, I had watched Mum bake bread, shouldn't be too difficult, and I wouldn't go hungry working in the bakery.

The Russian troops continued to pass the camp all day, all going toward Berlin. By the afternoon, in spite of the SBO's instructions, private foraging parties were out looking for food. We made a short excursion round the outside of the camp, leaving one of the combine to take care of our belongings. Tomorrow we would venture further.

TUESDAY 24TH APRIL: THE RUSSIANS TAKE OVER
Those assigned to the orderly room had found all the POW records. These were distributed to each man, "Derfonalfarte" (Personal Records). We were given two cards each.

The gates were manned by RAF linguists, but we passed in and out the camp without hindrance.

During the morning the Russian Admin types arrived, they assumed control of the camp, took over the admin offices. It was fortunate we had been given our personal records. They issued their first order, "No one to leave the camp."

Their admin was more bureaucratic than ours or the Germans. Mainly women, all butch types, wearing the same uniform as the men. Next order "Everyone has to register." This registering was to take some days, we queued awaiting our turn. Name, Rank, Number, age, and home address.

In the meantime the wire the tanks had crushed was fixed back into position, we were virtual POWs again.

A Russian film crew arrived, we were told to line the fence and wave as the camera passed by. This we did with some gusto, but some thought we should have ignored the cameras,

I went over to see Sly, (Bruce Cunningham) he had been out earlier on a foraging party. He along with others had found a field planted with seed potatoes. They had systematically gone through the field, recovering every potato. Sly had finished with 35 small ones, which by the time I called on him were cooked and ready for eating. Whilst we talked, he ate every last one, skin and all. I didn't ask for one, but if offered I wouldn't have said no. Such was the way of POW life.

THE LONG WAIT: WE NEED MORE FOOD
It looked as though we would have a long stay in the camp under Russian control. There was talk of being sent home via Odessa. By days 3 & 4, several bods had decided to leave, try to make their way to the American lines, somewhere to the South West.

We ignored the "Not to leave camp" order. We ventured out, foraging, the official parties were doing well, but we wanted to supplement our diet.

One day, the foraging party brought in a beast, worse for wear than we were, thin, the ribs sticking out like barrel hoops, it was last seen in the kitchen compound.

On our first foraging party, we came across a farm, no damage to the buildings, we walked inside, to find a dozen Frenchmen sitting around the table being served dinner by the farmer and his wife. The French objected to our intrusion, apparently, they had worked on the farm and throughout the war had enjoyed a good life. After threats from both sides we managed to get some eggs. We scoured the barn yard for more eggs, found a few, these were the first eggs we had since leaving England.

We walked to Jutterbug in the afternoon, just a little to the south. We took coffee to swap, knocked on doors, but the people were too frightened to answer. Russians, mainly women, patrolled the streets in their red uniforms. There were signs of a skirmish in the village, shell holes in some buildings.

Eventually we found a house with a small yard, chickens in the yard, small and skinny, no meat on them. I was for taking them, the old man of the house shook in his boots. Gilly, soft hearted Gilly, felt sorry for him, so we left without the chickens.

At one house, our knock was answered. Gilly who had taken German lessons in Luft VII spoke to them. We offered them coffee, they were delighted, the man, his wife, son and daughter tasted Nescafe for the first time. The eight of us passed the afternoon away, Gilly doing his best, they were pleased we were not Russians.

We made our way back to camp, Mike and others awaiting our booty, we had none, but we had left a little goodwill with a crushed people.

DEAD RUSSIAN PILOT IN PLANE

A hidden arms cache had been found in the forest nearby. We explored the path near where the arms had been found. It was great to walk the paths in the pine forest, real freedom. In a clearing we came across a crashed Russian plane, the pilot dead alongside his aircraft, we left him there, for there was little we could do. We found the arms cache, a pit maybe 5 yards by 5 yards and very deep. Bods were digging, finding pistols, machine guns and grenades, obviously had been hidden by German troops. I wasn't keen to hang about, if one grenade had gone off, the whole forest would have gone up. We were too close to home to take risks now. There was no advantage in carrying arms.

AN OFFICER FISHING

One expedition I did on my own to Luckenwalde, I came across an old sandpit, full of water. On the bank was an RAF bod fishing, trying his luck with a bent pin. I went over to him to ask the usual question "Had any luck?". To my surprise it was Donahue, the F/Lt I had shared a cell with in Antwerp. We exchanged a few words, but I got the impression he wasn't keen on talking to other ranks. I thought "Snobby Bastard," and left. I mentioned the whereabouts of the pond to a couple of army types I met. They told me it had been fished out with hand grenades. I laughed when I thought of that bloke at the end of the line with a bent pin.

28TH APRIL: ATTEMPTING TO BREAK CAMP

On the 28th, we decided to break camp, make for the Elbe. The Russians would not or could not give any news of what was to happen to us. Every day we watched German troops, now Russian prisoners, being marched, trotted, and run past the camp, in utter humiliation, all on their way to Russia. We began to think this would happen to us. So we decided to be our own masters. We packed all we could carry, food, clothes, blankets. We left at first light, leaving Mike Harrington and one or two others behind, they were either sick or felt the venture too risky. Our plan was to head south and then west to the Elbe. We took the railway line out of Luckenwalde that headed south, no fear of trains, all transport had come to a stop. It was a fine day, we felt free and began to enjoy ourselves. By noon we had covered some miles and were in a cutting with a high embankment either side. All of a sudden, we heard and almost felt rifle and machine gun fire, it was close enough to smell the cordite burning. The firing came just ahead and above us. Had we been exposed we would have copped the lot. Whoever was firing didn't know we were in the cutting. We scuttled to the side of the tracks and tucked into the embankment. We wondered what to do next. Whilst in the cutting we appeared to be safe, the cutting went on for some distance. Could we get through without being seen, should we stay or go back? After some discussion, we decide to retrace our steps and have another go tomorrow. We had to admit failure.

It was late evening when we returned to camp, our floor spots were still free, Mike had kept them for us.

An officer came into the barracks, he called out a list of names, mine was on the list, it was a list of tradesmen required for various duties. I was needed for the bakery, I told the officer Fred Brown had left that day, so I wouldn't be called again. I was keener to get out of camp than work in a bakery.

EAGER TO GET HOME

Next day we couldn't make up our minds what to do, whether to leave or not, I wanted to be on my way. I went to the Yank compound to ask if any of their men were leaving. There was some excitement in the compound, a reporter had got through the Russian lines in a jeep. He was in the Yank orderly room getting a story. A crowd surrounded the jeep, awaiting the reporter to return, I guess I was the only RAF bod there. Whilst we waited, a Yank forced open a box in the jeep, it contained the reporter's rations, chocolate, cigarettes. Much to the disgust of his mates, he stole the lot. I was shocked, taking a man's rations like that. The reporter told us the Yanks were at the Elbe and didn't intend crossing the river. He would report on our living conditions and see if he could get transport to pick us up.

The days passed by, we seemed bogged down. There were skirmishes around the camp, the Germans putting up a fierce fight. We heard of the fighting in Berlin, the war hadn't finished yet.

Rumours persisted about our release, but it seemed we were to go home through Russia.

We listened to the BBC, no need to hide the sets now, enough sets to have one or two in each barrack, sets no doubt taken from nearby houses.

We explored the district looking for anything of use. One day we met one of our old guards. He was old, out of uniform now, he had been one of the better guards, we spoke with him, he told us he was living close to the camp, and with luck would miss the trip to Russia.

LATE AFTERNOON 7TH MAY: ESCAPE AT LAST

I was on my usual scrounge, going from compound to compound. I was with the Yanks when a truck pulled in. The first Allied vehicle to reach the camp. I stood and listened, the driver was talking to the Yanks. I heard they would be prepared to take a truck load of men back to the Elbe. So without further ado I dashed back to tell Chappie & Co. Told them what I heard. Did they want to go? They hesitated, I grabbed my Yank greatcoat, left all my other gear and was on the way back to the truck. A friend, Ray Griffiths, had heard what I said, he was with me, hadn't taken him long to make up his mind. We managed to get on the truck, what excitement.

Soon we were on the move, in a couple of hours we were at the Elbe. What a welcome sight. There was a temporary bridge across the river, about 200 yards long. After some chat with the Russians and shouts across the river, we crossed and were in Allied territory. The truck took us to Magdeburg, the Yanks had an HQ there.

Tired, happy, but very very hungry, we were told, at a factory close by, the Yanks had a mess, we would be able to get a meal there. Trouble was, when we got there, every liberated POW in the area knew about the mess. We joined the queue that snaked around a large hall, this was going to take a time, the queue moved ever so slowly. It was now late into the night, we could see the kitchen staff working like slaves at the far end of the hall. We just had to be patient, no breaking the line, anyway, there was nothing else to do. After a couple of hours we made it to the serving counter, bacon, eggs, and ice cream, this was living. Having nowhere to sleep we joined the queue again.

The American Quartermaster began to complain, all his rations were going and his staff had to have a break. From the Yanks who were in the queue, he got a reception he wouldn't forget, he continued to serve throughout the night. We eventually got a second serve. By now it was daylight, we explored the factory looking for a place to sleep. We found one of our old barrack mates, Roberts from Liverpool, he had found a typewriter in one of the offices, said he was taking it home for his niece. We laughed, all we wanted was to get home in one piece.

BUT HOW TO GET HOME?

We rested, then took a look round Magdeburg or some of it. We wondered what to do, where to go, there was no organization to help us. More trucks arrived bringing in ex Stalag IIIA men, we met Chappie and the rest of the combine, just 24 hours behind us. We told them where to get a feed. Chappie had all my gear, he said I didn't deserve it. I agreed, took my diary and POW papers, gave him the rest. That is the last time I saw Chappie. Had we known, we would have said much more.

Someone told us, that there was an airfield at Brunswick, not too many miles away, it was being used to ferry POWs home. Early next morning Ray and I set out to find the airfield. We knew it was to the west. We found the autobahn, no pedestrians allowed, but we walked along the side trying to thumb a lift. Yankee trucks going our way, but none slowed down. Then we realized why, in our ill-clad dishevelled state, we looked like refugees. We walked to a turn off, and waited for a truck to slow down on the turn. We shouted at the first truck to turn off the autobahn. It went, some distance away it stopped, the driver recognized the accents. "You English?" he shouted, "Yes," running toward the truck. We told him who we were, what we wanted to do. He and his mates said they couldn't help, but confirmed there was an airfield at Brunswick airlifting POWs. They took a K Pack ration out of the truck, took the cigarettes out, gave us the rest, enough food for weeks. What food, tinned bacon and eggs, chocolate, we fed by the roadside, stored as much as we could carry in our packs.

It took a time, but eventually we got a lift to Brunswick. We walked to the airfield, it had been a permanent Luftwaffe base, brick built barracks, every convenience.

We reported to a very busy clerk, who took our names, then told us which barrack to report to. It had been a busy exciting day, we dropped our kit on a bed. I said to Ray that I would have a scout around to see if there was any food going.

INSTANT 'PROMOTION'

In the distance I could see a DC3 being loaded on the tarmac, a queue of men going aboard, I went to see what was going on. There was a Yank in charge, organizing the men climbing on board. I asked "How do you get aboard one of these aircraft?" He told me this was the last flight of the day, all aircraft were full. He then said "If you are an officer, I can get you a flight on this one." It was the quickest field promotion ever. I told him I was an officer. I was told "You have ten minutes to grab your gear." I flew back to the room, told Ray I had got a lift, picked up my gear and was away. Ray later told me everyone in the room was upset, that they hadn't got a lift that night. I was last aboard. I had a position facing the rear hatch, only the rear hatch was not closed, this I was told was a safety measure. It was a hair-raising experience, I hung on to the fuselage all the way. We passed over some glorious country, superb scenery. The Yank pointed out the Siegfried Line. I had no idea where we were bound. Late that night we landed on a temporary airfield in Northern France, it was 10th May. On our arrival we were allocated to areas, forms to sit on, coffee but no food. I sat with a couple of army types, they had been POWs for sometime. We sat and talked through the night. We were to be shipped out the following afternoon.

11TH MAY: NORTHERN FRANCE AND THEN HOME!

In the morning we decided to have a walk around the village, no point in just sitting and waiting. We carried all our gear with us, didn't want to lose anything at this stage.

There was nothing of interest in the village, we decided to ask one of the locals to brew us a coffee. A lady answered a door we had knocked on. She invited us in, and was about to make a brew of ersatz coffee. We said "No," and gave her a large tin of Nescafe. She was beside herself and had to explain to her two young children what it was, the only coffee they had tasted was the ersatz kind.

They marvelled at the taste, we thanked them and left them the coffee and all the other rations we were carrying.

Back to the airfield, we had lots of time to kill. We watched the Yanks moving German POWs, this was something we savoured. Some Germans were being loaded onto a big Yankee truck. The Germans complained, that there were too many on the truck.

My thoughts went back to the crowded cattle trucks. None of us had any sympathy for the Hun. We had all suffered at their hands. The next scene was a delight to watch, especially for this ex-captive audience. The truck driver pulled away along the tarmac, gathering speed, then applied the pneumatic brakes, all those aboard were swept toward the front of the truck, now there was room for as many again. We cheered encouragement to the driver.

Early afternoon, we were marshalled along the edge of the runway, numbered off, into aircraft loads. In came the Lancasters, squadrons of them, tears came to my eyes. Such a stirring sight. As an aircraft came to rest, a batch of men would board. When it came to our turn, again tears and a lump in my throat, the aircraft letters, JI my squadron, 514 squadron Waterbeach. I spoke to a member of the crew, told him I was 514, he took me up front, I sat alongside the navigator. The deck of the Lanc was numbered, just enough space for each man to squat a number.

I was given a spare headset, I passed it to one of the army lads, who would never have heard aircrew on intercom before. Take off, the French coast, the White cliffs of Dover, Vera Lynn, tears again. A beautiful day, our destination Ford near Brighton. The date May 11th 1945. I had been away just a year to the day.

Ron Rickard

ELSIE BONHAM'S BROTHER

Ron Rickard (left)

WORKING LIFE BEFORE JOINING THE FORCES

I was in the 64th Company, Royal Engineers attached to the 7th Armoured Brigade.

Prior to joining up I worked at the Halton Camp and biked from Mentmore to Halton to be there at 8am. On one occasion by a brook on the Long Marston Road there was a Wellington aircraft right across the road. I checked no one was in it and went in a field to get round it.

During the war I also worked on Cheddington airfield extending the runways for G. Walker Slater. I joined the war late, in 1943, because I had been in a reserved occupation and was working on radar. After a row with my boss at Halton I decided I would prefer a job in the forces.

TRAINING IN THE INFANTRY

I trained in the Infantry at York and was sent to Ripon on a crash course to drive transporters. Some weighed 73 tons with a tank on top. The tanks were usually Shermans, but sometimes a Churchill, but we were trained to fight alongside the infantry if required, as happened near Osnabruck in Germany. We moved up to support the Oxford and Bucks and Canadians to repel an effort by the enemy to close the top of the horse-shoe which would have trapped thousands of troops. Luckily they were repelled before we were needed.

VE DAY AT CLOPPENBURG

On VE Day morning we were at Cloppenburg, Germany. On the eve of VE Day we were all supplied with a bottle of Whitbread's beer, we knew that the war was coming to an end. We all said "Cheers" and went to bed. In the night I was woken by Captain Wilson who said "Wake up Rickard we've got a job."

We were ordered to go through the night to an experimental airfield at Jever near Wilhelmshaven to stop any destruction of evidence on secret equipment. They wanted to see what the German equipment was made of. There were seven in our group which left Cloppenburg for the airfield. The journey was over 100 kilometres through occupied Germany. We had a White Scout car (armoured car), a 15 cwt Bedford and a jeep.

ARRIVAL AT JEVER AIRFIELD

I was Captain Wilson's driver and I drove him into the airfield in the jeep. When we arrived at the airfield there were two Luftwaffe guards on the gate. They looked disinterested, they knew the war was ending within hours. Captain Wilson got out of the jeep and said to them "Stand at one side chaps will you."

The airfield was a very neat and impressive sight – entrance with shrubs and flowers – a peacetime Luftwaffe airfield.

As we approached the airfield we could see that it was newly tarmacadamed, we found these two guards on the gate, Luftwaffe chaps, who were quite disinterested knowing the war was ending within hours and so they just shrugged and let us through. I had been trained to look out for blemishes or pockmarks in the tarmac as these indicated that a mine could be underneath. We tried to avoid any possible mines by driving very gingerly in a dog leg fashion. The Captain did not realise that the pockmarks were a sign of mines. (We later discovered that five mines had been picked up from this airfield, two were powerful 'S' mines made of plastic and wood and therefore undetectable by a mine detector.) I spent every day up there for almost a week with the officer.

Lance Sergeant Clough was killed demonstrating the S mine diffusing to the Company. In peace time he was a professional footballer. We often wondered whether the footballer, and later manager, Clough was any relative.

THE COMMANDANT'S HOUSE

He decided that we should look at the house on the right, which was very imposing - a big detached house. He said that would be the Commandant's accommodation, which he was dead right. We went there and of course the door was locked. We banged on the door, we kicked it, we did everything, rang the bell - no answer. So he said "Right Rickard and Scott," - funny thing was the corporal's name was Peter Scott, you remember the bird man, well same name as him. We used to call him 'birdie'. But anyway Scott and I put our shoulders to the door. In fact it looked like a very strong oak door but in fact it was only a made up thing because it went in like splinter you know and we finished up in the hallway on our backs. Anyway we got up and he said "You all right Rickard?" I said "Yeh we're fine." So he said "Right anybody at home?" and of course he's shouting out "Anybody here?" And of course there's no answer and I felt the Aga, there was an Aga cooker there, and that was red hot nearly. So I said "There's somebody about the cooker's well going," and all of a sudden 'bomp bomp,' somebody got out of bed and this chap come down the stairs, and you wouldn't believe it, he spoke such perfect Oxford English. He come strutting down there fully dressed and he'd got khaki uniform on, which was SS with a swastika armband and anyway he said "Good morning gentlemen, war is over, yes?" So Wilson the

Captain looked at him and said "Yes." So he said "And what can I do for you"? "If you'll step down here sir." So he come down. Wilson first of all looked at him and he said "Can I first of all ask you what you are doing, an SS man in charge of an airfield?" He said "Of course you know don't you." And Wilson said "What do you mean I know?" So Wilson said "How would I know? What do you mean I know" He said "Well you know it's a very secret airfield like your Farnborough." He knew all about Farnborough. Scotty Yorkie and Smudger were sent to cut the phone wires outside

Wilson said "Frisk him." The Commandant said "No need, I have a gun." It was a 45 millimetre Luger (which in later years I handed in to Linslade Police Station). I grabbed the gun out of the holster and frisked him. I found a small Luger, a tiny Derringer type, under his arm pit. He hadn't mentioned that!

Wilson ordered "Cut the phone lines and take the cable with you. Make sure they can't join them up again."

The Commandant asked "How many are you?" We replied hundreds, tanks on the far side and paratroops forward (remember we were just seven!). We had to bluff or we would have been captured. He said "Quite a strong force then."

We took two revolvers from the house. The officer Wilson said "Rickard you can have the big one, I want the little one."

(After the war at about three year intervals, there were amnesties granted to anyone who handed in any weapons that were obtained. I handed mine in on the third amnesty at Linslade police station to Inspector King.)

I asked the Captain if we could take the radio to enable us to hear the celebration party in London. he said "If I turn round and it's gone I wouldn't know." I also took a Telefunken portable radio so that we could hear the BBC. We had it tuned to the BBC Foreign Service, and while some of the inmates from the prison camp were in there, as their language came up they clapped, laughed and hugged us as they heard what was happening. Wherever I went after that I took it and we could hear the jollifications in London. That finished up at Mentmore.

THE AIRFIELD

The airfield had radar controlled anti-aircraft guns in four barrels in concrete dugouts at four points of the airfield. There were Messerschmitts 163 (little rockets with a flight endurance of 10 minutes, they could climb to a terrific height, the same as flying fortresses flying high).

They had a map on the wall and one of England – all dotted in red. Glasgow was gonna get a terrific pasting – there were lots of red dots. On the map of Germany there was a surrounding area where these little rockets, Messerschmitts 163, could land as they had only a ten minutes fuel flying duration.

On the airfield there were a dozen Messerschmitts 110 fighter bomber fitted with radar in the nose, with four aerials pointing forward. There were so many things there – aircraft, radar controlled guns and radar installations. We found one hangar with a type of NAAFI with a counter and beer underneath. The officer, Wilson, said "I don't know if I should let you drink it. Scotty had already drunk some, he said it tasted like sweet stout. Wilson said "No, you can come back for it."

The airfield was constructed to look like a farm and painted like hayricks. From the air they would look like hayricks. The runway was 18 inches thick of concrete, then covered with turf and a heavy wire mesh binding the lot together. They had cows on there sometimes. The landing lights were portable. There were thousands of them. One was used as a light by the bed.

NEXT DAY

At 5am the next morning it began to get light in the two big Nissen huts with the chimney smoking. They were full of Luftwaffe staff – girls and men. Everyone said "Good morning." One girl asked "Would you like some breakfast?" I was starving. The officer, knew I was always hungry, made us refuse the offer. . Upstairs there were all little box rooms which were quarters for the girls. We were all given notepads to jot down what we saw.

Wilson said "I want to look in all these map cabinets. You can look in the next hangar." It was a long way to the other side of the airfield. I drove to the hangar and found 30 Luftwaffe blokes having a pep talk from their officer on what was gonna happen in three hours time. I got out of the jeep and there was some sniggering. I said to them "I understand completely what you are saying." I hadn't got a clue but they shut up like a clamp. Again they asked how many of us there were. Of course I told them what we'd told the Commandant

There was a Junkers 88, a fast attack bomber with an experimental gun, in the hangar. In my bluff and now in front of 150-200 people, I climbed up the inspection steps and tried to look intelligent. An officer broke away and saluted me. "What have we got to do,? he asked.

I replied "Remain here." He asked how many we were. I said "We have tanks on the far side and paratroops forward and infantry to the rear." I told them to remain there until they heard from the officer.

RETRIEVING THE BEER

I returned to Wilson and asked if we could get the beer. He told us to go round by road so Corporal Scott and myself drove the two or three miles to pick up the beer. We found a ladder and rolled one of the barrels up the ladder on top of the jeep in the spare wheel well. We started moving along the road which was pock marked with shell holes. Scott, who was driving, was getting thrown about violently. My arms were aching holding the barrel. There was a sudden lurch and I ended up in the ditch with the barrel. The bung came out of the barrel and the beer spouted out, we cut a bung made from the hedgerow and used it to stop the flow.

We got back to the huts with the beer. Captain Wilson came out of the hut. He said "I have two bottles of wallop, a bottle of whisky and a bottle of gin. It's my birthday, which one do you want?" He gave the chaps the gin. He advised us not to try the beer in case it was doped.

ARRIVAL OF DISPLACED PERSONS

We heard a clamour outside, people were banging on the door. There were hundreds of people outside. The huts we were in were prisoner of war camps for displaced persons – they were starving. They came from Latvia, Estonia, Poland and Yugoslavia. They repeated "Kameraden, kameraden" and kissed us. We said that we weren't having them in the huts, but they came in a few at a time. We gave them a drink of the beer. Amongst them were two Americans, they could hardly walk, they said "We're from California, can anyone speak English? We are in a working camp." We asked "What are these huts?" They said that they were for the German guards and that they had cleared off when they saw the Brits.

A SHOWER AT LAST – BUT AT WHAT COST?

We had not had a bath for weeks. By this time of course the war had been officially declared over. Captain Wilson went off in the jeep to see the town Burgomaster (or Mayor as we would know them). There were three big overhead water tanks on brick piers – also some of the boys had been taking weapons that had been handed in so we decided they wouldn't need an airfield anymore. So we grabbed a couple of German Schmeissers and fired at the tanks. Everyone stripped off and had the luxury of a shower. When the Captain drove in he said "Great," and also stripped off to shower, then turned round and said "How the hell are you going to stop it?" We got a severe reprimand and told we were very lucky to get away with it. They put it down to exuberance at the signing of the Armistice.

In later years in the sixties, a lad from Mentmore was doing his National Service (two years) and I asked him where he was stationed and he said "Jever near Wilhelmshaven." I said "Did you notice the big water tanks at the far side of the drome?" He said he did, and I asked if he saw any patches on the smaller one. He said "Yes it had orange patches all over it." And I told him how it came about – apparently the tanks didn't only supply the drome, but a large part of the town of Jever. We were lucky no action was taken.

FINDING A CAR FOR CAPTAIN WILSON

The next morning in an exuberance of victory Wilson went to see the burgomaster of the town. On his return he said "The old man, the major, has confiscated an Opel (a big limousine)." The Adjutant had got a Ford Taunus. Wilson said "I want to get one to beat all of them."

Down the side of the airfield there were some lovely detached houses and a long row of Luftwaffe garages. Wilson and I broke into the garages. A young man came hobbling up on crutches, he had been a Messerschmitt fighter pilot. He pleaded "Please do not taking car." It was an invalid car supplied by the Luftwaffe with a DKW engine set round the back axle. We assured him we would not take it. We came to another big Opel. It had a white sheet over it. We couldn't take it because it had a steering lock. We found one with German camouflage painting on it. It was used by a senior person on the airfield. It was a French Lascelle, a straight eight cylinder, with a huge bonnet. I tried to start it. Wilson wanted to take this one back to show off with. We towed it onto the airfield. When I lifted the boot up it had lots of little packs of charcoal, a burner in the middle. It had been converted from petrol to a gas producer – hence the little bags of charcoal. I tried to light the fire with the charcoal but I couldn't get it to go. I didn't understand the gas producer. I lashed the Fieseler Storch tank onto the roof. I made a gravity feed with piping into the carburettor. I made jets from wood. The car drove beautifully when Wilson came in at night, he asked how it was going. I replied that I had got the car going after a fashion. It started on a fast tick over but it wouldn't tick over slowly. It drove like a Rolls Royce over the shell holes. Scotty drove it back to Cloppenburg. I was mad because I had done all the work. Captain Wilson said I want you to come round in the morning with the car and announce in a very pompous way "Captain Wilson, your car is without." Several officers gathered round admiring the car. The major asked if we were going for a ride. The Major, two Captains, and three Lieutenants sat in the back of the car and smoked cigars and drank wine. I was in the front driving with an officer. After we had driven about 80 miles a Captain in the Royal Army Service Corps (RASC) stopped the vehicle and asked "Is this a German vehicle?" He said he was impounding it. By then we were within four miles of our camp. The RASC Captain took the Major and Adjutant, the rest of us had to walk the four miles back. We were billeted in Siemens' factory in Spandau, a Berlin suburb, with the Russians.

STARVING CHILDREN IN BERLIN

We went from Cloppenburg to Berlin, a journey of over 100 miles on the autobahn in a convoy which stretched two miles. We were the 21st Army Group made up of Canadian and British. We carried a huge amount of equipment. We stopped two miles short of going into the city. Haversack rations were handed out by the cooks – then from nowhere there appeared a couple of dozen children offering berries – hoping for something better in return, so we gave out what we could. When we got into Berlin we saw starving children. One chap gave a child food off his plate. Then they all started taking a child and giving them food. The 'Old Man' said "Stop this! We have rations to feed one company not the whole of Berlin." So the cooks scrubbed the bins and separated our leftovers into first course and desserts for the children to eat. Woe betide you if you left the lid off. The cooks said "Put that lid back on," because the children were starving.

SPANDAU

Yorkie and I walked beyond Spandau to the centre and it was a mass of ruins. We found a Russian soldier trapped underneath a girder. We released him and then chaired him the two or three miles back to Spandau. He was from Spandau and stationed at Siemens' factory, as we were. We made our own billets and I slept on a chaise longue. I got lice and had to be deloused the next morning.

THE RUSSIANS

The Russians went into the fields for food. We saw them driving a cow through Berlin and they tried to kill it with an axe. An officer came out and shot the cow and it was cooked in a portable copper. It smelled beautiful. Russian girl soldiers directed the traffic through the city with red, white and green flags. A Russian woman soldier had a bandolier of cartridges round her. Wrighty and I went to meet her and she pulled a gun on us. She was very security conscious. The Russian Sergeant Major received the wounded soldier and he gave us a cup of coffee. We went to Unter-Den-Linden, Hitler's favourite night club.

REICHSTAG AND REICH CHANCELLERY

Members of the Company were sent to Reichstag and Reich Chancellery to show a presence that the British were there. We were based at Spandau near Hess's prison at Potsdam. The Russians were in control of Berlin, they had been there for a week. I was part of a reconnaissance group. When I got to the Reich Chancellery, which was the place where Goebbels poisoned the children and then shot himself, I saw a place outside the ruins which had been blackened by fire and I discovered that it was the place where Hitler's and Eva Braun's bodies were burned.

BRANDENBURG GATE

One day I took Captain Wilson to a meeting in the city. When I returned to collect him I went through the Brandenburg Gate and got lost as there was so much damage. I was stopped by four Russian officers and escorted to the meeting place. Captain Wilson told me he had a very important task, he had been ordered to act as Reception Officer to receive 'Heads of State' who were to arrive at Gatow airfield. These were Trueman, Attlee, De Gaulle, Stalin, and General Sikorski (Polish). As we approached the airfield, about every 500 yards, there was a very smart Russian soldier who stood to attention and saluted us by pushing their rifles forward and standing astride. The Captain explained that as he had no other transport other than my jeep, he wanted me to 'get lost' and return every twenty minutes in case he wasn't provided with any other transport. I was asked if I saw these VIPs. I said "Of course I saw them, but at a distance, then only a brief glimpse."

The VIPs were provided with limousines, I think they were Russian. The Captain rode back with one of them and I had to return alone being saluted all the way down the autobahn.

RETURN TO ENGLAND

We came back to England on tank transporters or Landing Ship Tanks (LSTs). We left at Calais and arrived at Dover. I nearly threw the gun in the sea because there was an announcement that "Anyone found with German arms as souvenirs would be returned to their units and Court Martialled. I packed it in the middle of my kitbag and risked it!

VICTORY PARADE

We took part in the Victory Parade through London. I remember we were billeted in Kensington Gardens, our tent was right by Peter Pan's statue.

On the morning of the parade we formed up in our different regiments. Raymond Glendenning, the news commentator, was flying in a Lancaster over Hyde Park and he was controlling the order of departure. The Colonel of the Grenadier Guards felt they should lead, but the Royal Engineers was the oldest regiment. So, after a brief discussion, it was agreed the Grenadiers should lead. As we marched off a company from Kenya marched right across our lines – this caused a problem until Raymond Glendenning put things back in order. As we marched into Parliament Square, from the large buildings overhead came a shower of cigarettes, sweets etc., but for a start we were at 'Attention', but when the Brigadier gave the 'Stand Easy' we were allowed to pick them up. Also we passed the Royal Dais down the Mall, we were given the 'Eyes Right' and we all said about the Royal Family wearing some sort of make-up, I suppose for the cameras.

Appendix I

EXTRACTS FROM THE MINUTES OF THE CHEDDINGTON PARISH COUNCIL MEETINGS

January 13th 1941

Mr. Boarder brought to the notice of the Council of Evacuated families residing in Andrews Terrace depositing ashes and refuse in ditches and the clerk* was instructed to bring this to the notice of the Wing R.D. Council. *R.H.Tompkins

July 21st 1941

The chairman read a Circular letter he had received from the Leighton Linslade and Wing R.D. Council re War weapons Week Aug. 2nd – 9th 1941. The Council decided to call a representative meeting of the Parish to consider this. G. Alcock. Aug 15th 1941

August 17th 1941

The Clerk presented a Circular Letter he had received from the Wing R.D.C. re Local Defence Committees together with a covering letter from the Bucks C.C. which stated that the Committee should be constituted as follows:

The Senior Officer of the Home Guard

The Senior Police Officer

The Senior Warden

The Food Organiser

The Council after discussion approved the committee and instructed the Clerk to reply to that effect.

December 16th 1941

The Clerk produced a Circular Letter received from the Wing R.D. Council re the Salvaging of Iron Railings Etc. and after careful consideration the Clerk was instructed to write to the Wing R.D. Council as follows. That the Parish Council unanimously agreed, that they would prefer the Wing R.D. Council appoint a competent person to make the survey and prepare the schedule. G. Alcock, Chairman

February 15th 1943

A letter from the Bucks War Agricultural Executive Committee Wing District, asking the Parish Council their views on the matter of Ploughing the Recreation ground, as this had been suggested to the Committee. The Council decided unanimously not to entertain this suggestion and instructed the Clerk to answer their letter to that effect.

March 8th 1943

The Chairman read a letter he had received re Wings for Victory Week May 22nd – 29th 1943 asking that a public meeting be called. The council decided that this meeting should be held on Monday March 22nd 1943 at 8p.m. Mr Jeffery kindly promises to get out the notices.

October 4th 1943

Correspondence. Ministry of Health
1. A Circular letter no 2835 re Contracts of Local Authorities.
2. 2. A letter from the Wing Rural District Council re Post War housing needs.

The Council resolved to ask for ten houses in the first year after the War and ten more spread over the following four years. Suitable sites being New Street, Church Lane and High Street south of and adjoining Town Farm.

January 15th 1945

Vacant allotments. The Allotment Committee reported that 95 allotments were let & £11.13.2 paid leaving 6 vacant. It was unanimously agreed to leave the matter with the Committee & if necessary to let the vacant lots free for a year if tenants could be found.

An application from the Clerk that his salary should be increased to £10 per ann. as was paid to his predecessor, was considered.

Parish Meeting Mr F.S. Jeffery introduced the matter of preparing the Welcome Home of Service men and women after Hostilities were finished & suggested the Parish Council should call a Parish Meeting to consider the matter.

November 5th 1945

New Council Houses. This matter was looked into and after a long discussion it was agreed that a letter be sent to Wing Rural District Council pointing out that this Council was gravely concerned at the delay in the post-war housing programme for this Parish and if the parish was not kept in line with the programme of neighbouring parishes they will be compelled to address their protest to the Ministry of Health. A week to be given for a satisfactory reply.

Prop. Mr Beasley   Sec. Mr Tompkins carried unanimously.

War Memorial The name of the Parish on the War Memorial was taken off for war defence purposes and it was decided that the Chairman should get in touch with the proper authority to have this replaced in time for Remembrance Day.

Prop. Mr Tompkins Sec. Mr Wesley carried unan.

Appendix II

WARTIME EXTRACTS FROM THE LEIGHTON BUZZARD OBSERVER

Extract from the Leighton Buzzard Observer 25th July 1939 cont

WING RURAL DISTRICT COUNCIL

BLANKETS COMING
The Ministry of Health notified the Council that 450 blankets were to be sent to the district. The Clerk pointed out that these were a quarter of what was required. A hundred yards of mackintosh sheeting is being sent.

GET IN SUPPLIES
Another circular from the Home Office appealed to householders to get in one week's supply of food. Mr Edmunds: Do you give them a cheque to buy it then? (Laughter)

INCREASING PRODUCTION
Asking if there were a possibility of increasing production rather than controlling food, Mr. Hawkins said that people ought to be asked to do more on the allotments in various parishes. Only half the allotments were let and they were only half as well done.   The Rev. C.W. Morris said that some of the money being spent should be given in prizes for allotments.

Extract from the Leighton Buzzard Observer 25th July 1939

WING RURAL DEFENCE
L.C.C. LORD ROSEBERY'S OFFER
REFUGEES RATIONS ARRIVING

The rejection by the London County Council of the Earl of Rosebery's offer of Mentmore Stud to accommodate about a hundred handicapped children was reported to Wing Rural Council on Thursday.

The Clerk (Mr. M. C. Clifford) said that shortly after the last council meeting Mr. Edmunds met a L.C.C. schoolmaster and from the discussion it seemed that there would be no difficulty in getting authority from the L.C.C. to purchase the necessary equipment. Later a letter from the Chief Education Officer stated that he was unable to authorise expenditure on the work necessary to adapt the premises for the children and he had no alternative but to decline the offer.

Mr. Edmunds said the cost would have been about £150. The place would now be empty.

Speaking on the question of dealing with sick children, Mr. Edmunds said the gardener's Bothy could be used for sick children. It was isolated and could be used for sick children of other parishes.

Mr. Edmunds said the Youth Hostel at Ivinghoe was another ideal place.

Mr. Edmunds remarked that these two places could deal with the whole district.

RATIONS BEING SENT

The Food Defence Plans Department wrote that canned meat and milk would be forwarded to the refugee de-training points where there was most suitable storage accommodation. The canned meat and milk will come within a few days and other food will arrive shortly. The consignments will remain in the Station Master's charges.

OTHER A.R.P. MATTERS

There is some difficulty in finding a warden's post at Cheddington, but further inquiries are being made. The Organiser reported receiving a demonstration stirrup pump and that ten more would be provided. Mr. Lyon urged that further steps should be taken in fire fighting. The Committee agreed to purchase thirty stirrup pumps.

The committee have received a Home Office circular stating that the Committee should use their discretion in signing on people over the age limits for certain services providing they are fit.

Maroons and sirens, etc, are not to be used for summoning fire brigades in future as they are to be used for other purposes.

Extract from the Leighton Buzzard Observer 25th July 1939 Extract from The Leighton Buzzard Observer 12th September 1939

PETROL SUPPLIES

The clerk said that the use of petrol would be very restricted. Retailers would make their own arrangements for deliveries into the villages but they would not be allowed to go out with half-empty vans.

He had received no information as to the position of farm tractors and milk delivery vans.

Mr Morris: People using cars for national purposes can obtain extra supplies.

Extract from The Leighton Buzzard Observer 11th November 1942

CHEDDINGTON
WOMEN'S INSTITUTE

At the 15th annual meeting on Thursday the President (Mrs. Stoddart) was in the chair. The Secretary (Mrs Jeffery) read a report upon the year's activities which included the running of a sewing party (held at Ascott House), a savings association run by Mrs. Newton, all village salvage work, making camouflage netting for the army and a jam centre producing 700lb jam. A report upon the half yearly Council meeting was given by Mrs Jeffery. Next year's programme was arranged.

The social half hour was given up to a roll call of a saying or poem. The ballot resulted in the election of Mesdames Alcock, C. Bishop, Brindle, Hale, Hing, Jeffery, Mason, A. Perry, E. Perry, Stoddart, Towell, J. Wesley and President (Mrs Stoddart). The committee elected the other officers viz: President (Mrs Hale), Secretary (Mrs Jeffery), Assistant Secretary (Mrs. A. Perry), Treasurer (Mrs. Alcock), games (Mrs.Towell), Press correspondent (Mr. Bishop).

Extract from The Leighton Buzzard Observer 14th November 1942

MENTMORE EVACUEES
TOYS FROM LONDON FIREMEN AND
FIREWOMEN

Firemen and firewomen in "B" district of the London Fire Forces whose head quarters are at Euston have been making toys from timber salvaged after raids for children evacuated from London. This voluntary work is all done in their spare time.

The firemen and firewomen wished their work to go to places where the number of children could make use of the toys and on Tuesday a party of them visited

Mentmore Towers, the residence of Lord Rosebery which almost since the outbreak of the war has been used as a nursery for evacuee children. The "Blitzed

children" living there had one of the most exciting days of their lives. These fairy godfathers and godmothers were led by Mr. P.J. Thomas who mentioned that the work had been done under the auspices of the Children Welfare Association.

Many kinds of toys had been made including rocking horses, horses and carts, see-saws, bricks and other playthings likely to please children under five.   More than 150 toys were distributed, sufficient to give each child two toys and a large number over for general use. The children's delight can be imagined and the party were very warmly thanked for their work. The visitors were entertained to lunch and tea by the nursing staff and were then shown round the estate. They were particularly interested in "Blue Peter" which won the Derby for Lord Rosebery two years ago.

The party was welcomed by Dr. Norris of Aylesbury (Medical Supervisor), Mr. C.Edmunds and Miss Smith (Matron).

Appendix III

WARTIME EXTRACTS FROM CHEDDINGTON SCHOOL LOG - EVACUEES

Aug 28th, 1939   In accordance with instructions received in Circular 790 the staff of the school curtailed their holidays and returned for duty as required.

Sep 3rd, 1939   War was declared on Germany this morning. Arrangements for reopening the school on Sep 11th have been cancelled. The first evacuees reached Cheddington this morning.

Sep 19th, 1939   In accordance with instructions received in Circular 834 the school was opened for educational purposes this morning. By the exclusion of children under five years of age, and with the addition of a small quantity of extra furniture, it will probably be possible to amalgamate the evacuated children with those already on the school roll and organise the school for the full normal sessions.

Sep 20th, 1939   The total attendance at school yesterday was 96. Class I now numbers 38, Class II 30 and Class III 28. Of these 96 children, 37 are evacuees from various districts; and of the 37 evacuated children, 11 are evacuees under the Government scheme.

Sep 26th, 1939   Certain variations in numbers on the roll have occurred with the result that the total number on roll is now 89, of whom 7 are Government evacuees. Miss Davies of the Burghley School, Kentish Town N.W.5, reported for duty yesterday Sep 25th.

Oct 10th, 1939   Four K.G. tables and eight K.G. chairs have been supplied to accommodate the extra children in the Infants' class.

Nov 2nd, 1939   The number on roll is now 73 Bucks children and 10 government evacuees.

Nov 30th, 1939 A Staffing Return sent to the Education Office today showed the state of classes as:- Class I 31, Class II 27, Class III 24, Total 82.

Dec 1st, 1939 Average attendance for the week 69. The number of official evacuees is now 5.

Feb 9th, 1940 Miss D. Davies terminated her appointment to the school today, as circumstances no longer justify her retention, and she desires to return to London.

Jul 5th, 1940 The Summer Term ended this afternoon and a fourth term will commence on Monday next, covering the period to Sep 30th 1940. Ref Circ 506.

Aug 2nd, 1940 In accordance with instructions issued, the school closed this afternoon for a fortnight and will re-open on Monday, August 19th.

Sep 1st, 1940 Promotion of scholars was made this morning, the state of the classes is now Class I 23, Class II 23, Class III 16.

Sep 13th, 1940 Admissions during the week of evacuated children have made the number on roll 72.

Sep 17th, 1940 The school was closed for the purpose of instruction this afternoon as it was required for the reception of evacuees: staff in attendance.

Sep 19th, 1940 A party of fifty-two children has been drafted to the school: this party is on the charge of Mr C H Spary and is being merged into the Cheddington School until other arrangements can be made.

Sep 20th, 1940 The children of both groups i.e. local and officially evacuated have attended full sessions today. The weather has been fine enough for one class to be held outside, as inside accommodation is not sufficient for the whole of the children.
No. on roll:- Local and unofficial evacuees 78. Evacuated party 52.

Sep 23rd, 1940 Working arrangements continued as during end of last week, but difficulties have now arisen owing to bad weather.

Sep 26th, 1940 It has been found necessary to resort to dual arrangements today. By arrangement with Mr Spary the local children will attend afternoon sessions today and tomorrow, leaving the classrooms at the disposal of the evacuated party in the forenoon.

Oct 7th, 1940 School assembled this morning but no registration was made as the dual shift arrangements are still in operation, and the evacuated party is using the classrooms during the morning sessions this week.

Oct 8th, 1940 Arrangements having been made for use of the Church Room as supplementary accommodation, the dual shift system will terminate today: the evacuated party in the charge of Mr Spary and Mrs Donovan will use the Church Room exclusively, and the local children and unofficial evacuees will resume normal working in the school.

Oct 9th, 1940 A quantity of stock was transferred to Mr Spary from the school stock today.

Nov 1st, 1940 Numbers on school roll are now 112 plus 49 evacuees making a total of 161.

Nov 15th, 1940 Numbers on roll are now 109 plus 46 evacuees making a total of 155.

Nov 25th, 1940 In accordance with instructions received from the Education Office, merging of evacuee children with local children was carried out today. Fifteen evacuees will be transferred from the Church Room to the C. School premises: eight of these are over 12 yrs of age and seven are under 7 yrs. Eighteen children of ages 8 yrs to 11yrs inclusive will be sent to the Church Room from the C. School. By this arrangement there will be 44 children of ages between 7 yrs and 12 yrs at the Church Room and 101 children of all ages at the C. School. The three-class grouping will not be changed. The two LCC teachers, Mr C H Spary and Mrs Donovan, will be responsible for the class of 44 at C. Room.

Nov 29th, 1940 Numbers on roll have declined this week to 98 plus 38 evacuees, making a total of 136.

Dec 19th, 1940 The school closed this afternoon for the Christmas holidays. One teacher will be on duty each school day of the holidays to supervise the evacuee children who attend.

Mar 7th, 1941 Number on roll is now 88 local children and unofficial evacuees plus 34 official evacuees, i.e. 122.

Apr 28th, 1941 Miss N M Bodsworth terminated her seven years of service in the school today. No appointment has been made to fill the vacancy caused by her leaving.

May 9th, 1941 Mrs O Donovan has been transferred from the Church Room today to take charge of Class II. Mr C H Spary will remain at the Church Room with a class of 31 children.

May 16th, 1941 Mrs O Donovan having received permission to return to London terminated her appointment to the school staff today.

May 19th, 1941 Miss E M Limbrey (Unattached LCC teacher) commenced duties today as teacher for Class II.

May 22nd, 1941 Mr Waite, LCC H.M.I. visited the school today to make enquiries regarding the working conditions in the Church Room, and to get information needed to answer complaints and allegations made by the LCC teacher working there.

May 23rd, 1941 Re-organisation of classes was made this afternoon to take effect from Monday next. This school will now be divided into four classes of approximately 30 children. Infants will include children to 7½ yrs. Class III will include children 7½ to 9½ years and will be taught at the Church Room by Mr C H Spary. Class II will include children 9½ to 11½ yrs and will be taught by Miss Limbrey at the Council School. Class I will include all children over 11½ yrs and will be taught by the Headmaster.

Jul 9th, 1941 Arrangements have now been made for the girls at the Church Room to have a needlework lesson at the school on Mondays 2.15 - 3.15.

Jul 27th, 1941 Number on roll at the end of this quarter: Local & unofficial evacuees 85 Official evacuees 24.

Aug 25th, 1941 All scholars accommodated in Council School since Aug 18th.

Sep 15th, 1941 School reassembled this morning. ... Mr C H Spary has not returned to this school but no information has been received from the Education Officer regarding his transfer. Children grouped in the three classrooms at C. School under the supervision of headmaster and Miss Limbrey. No children at Church Room.

Oct 15th, 1941 A consignment of food and equipment for use if and when the school is needed as an Emergency Feeding and Rest Centre was delivered by the police this morning at 10 a.m.

Mar 31st, 1942 Registration for the year ending today was made as required on form 9E. The maximum number of children on roll during any week was 123; 89 local children and 34 official evacuees. This was the week ending April 25th 1941. The minimum number was 74: 61 local children and 13 official evacuees during the last month of the year.

Apr 1st, 1942 The LCC teacher, Miss E M Limbrey, who has been in charge of Class II, terminated her employment today as she has been recalled to London.

Apr 14th, 1942 School reassembled this morning after the Easter holidays. 74 children were present and as no teacher arrived to take Miss Limbrey's place, the whole school was put into two groups under the headmaster and Miss Alderman.

Apr 21st, 1942 Acting upon instructions from the Education Office Mrs F S Jeffery commenced work as Supply Teacher for Class II.

Apr 30th, 1942   A School Savings Group has been formed and affiliated to the National Savings Movement Its official number is 9E / 1 / 55.

Aug 7th, 1942   End of school year.

Aug 10th, 1942   Miss Alderman and Mrs Jeffery on duty today and until August 21st.   Headmaster on holiday during this period.

Aug 14th, 1942   An average of nine children attended during this week. They were given useful occupation in school and taken out for walks.

Aug 21st, 1942   About four children on average attended this week.

Aug 24th, 1942   Headmaster returned to duty. Three children present this morning.   Most boys are at harvest work with local farmers.

Aug 31st, 1942   No children present this morning. Teacher on duty spent the official times of opening, viz. 10 a.m. - 12 noon and 2 p.m. - 4 p.m. doing necessary work in the school garden.

Sep 7th, 1942   School opened this morning for the Autumn Term. Classes number 74 including evacuees of whom there are now 9.

Sep 11th, 1942 (SL)   Extra time has been spent in the school garden this week, while the girls have had needlework lessons..

May 22nd, 1943   Saturday: Children's Sports were held at the Manor House, by kind permission of Capt. L B Stoddart, as the opening event of "Wings for Victory" week.

Jun 16th, 1943   School re-assembled this morning. 55 children present out of 58. One other case of chicken pox has developed during the holiday.

Jul 1st, 1943   Miss WJ Alderman absent today, suspected to be suffering from chicken pox. Whole school placed under supervision of Headmaster.
Sep 6th, 1943   New term commenced this morning. Two children admitted and three taken off the roll.

For the current term only two classes will be formed. The Infants and St. 1 will be taught by Miss W J Alderman and the remainder of the school by the headmaster.   By this arrangement there will be 28 children in the lower section and 26 in the upper. Mrs Jeffery will continue part-time service three afternoons a week.

By means of money raised by the scholars, supplemented by a contribution from the Bridgewater Charity, and another contribution from the County Education Committee, an excellent Radio Receiving Set, costing £20, has been installed and arrangements have been made to use the BBC Schools Broadcasts this term.

Sep 10th, 1943   Numbers in the two classes are 24 and 26, not including 5 official evacuees.

Sep 27th, 1943   Alterations in the time table have been made to allow the introduction of the following BBC Broadcasts to Schools:

Singing together	Monday
11 - 11.30	
"Let's Join In"	Monday
11.45 - 12	
Music and Movement for Infants	Tuesday
11 - 11.30	
Physical Training	Tuesday
11.45 - 12	
Music and Movement for Juniors	Friday
11 - 11.30	

Oct 9th, 1943   A class of 10 girls is attending Linslade Girls' School on Fridays for a course in Domestic Instruction.

Nov 12th, 1943   As attendance for the week: 46. No. on books: 56 (4E)

Nov 19th, 1943   The girls attending Domestic Instruction Course at Linslade returned by train this afternoon, reaching Cheddington at about 6 p.m., as the bus failed to pick them up. Matter reported to Education Secretary.

Nov 23rd, 1943   Instruction received from Ed. Secy. to pay girls' railway fares and claim with postage.

Nov 29th, 1943 The Education Committee have approved a request made by the Headmaster to postpone the Christmas Holidays, making the dates of closure and reopening Dec 23rd and Jan 6th respectively instead of Dec 21st and Jan 4th. The change is made to enable the headmaster to attend a week's course at the Central School of Aircraft Recognition, Stockport, during the Christmas closure.

Dec 4th, 1943 A letter from the Ed Office states that the failure of the bus service on Nov 19th was unavoidable, and due to the sudden illness of the driver.

Jun 7th, 1944 By kind permission of Capt. L.B. Stoddart, a programme of children's sports was arranged at Cheddington Manor this evening in connexion with the "Salute the Soldier" week held throughout the W.R.D.C. this week.

Jul 4th, 1944 All gas-masks were inspected today, and arrangement made for changing wrong sizes.

Jul 20th, 1944 1350 books were collected by scholars during the last fortnight's "Book Drive" organised by the Wing.R.D.C. [Wing Rural District Council.]

Sep 11th, 1944 School re-opened this morning. Class I now consists of 34 children of ages 8 - 13 1/2 Class III 29 children. No children under 5 yrs of age have been admitted today.

Jan 12th, 1945 Staffing return shows two classes of thirty-one each on this date; of this number nine are official evacuees.

Mar 2nd, 1945 The Metropolitan Evac. Authy. Exam. was held today. Only one candidate, Geoffrey Church, was eligible for this exam.

Apr 17th, 1945 About 20 children were taken to Mentmore after school today to see the State Coach which has been stored there for safety during the war.

Apr 20th, 1945 Staffing Return sent to Ed. Office. This shows 68 on roll. Lower class 31 local and 4 O.E. Upper class 28 local, 5 O.E.

Apr 30th, 1945 Three unofficial evacuees were taken off register this morning.

May 7th, 1945 By an announcement from the BBC. at 8 p.m. this evening, tomorrow is officially proclaimed to be VE (Victory in Europe) Day. With this authority, the school will be closed tomorrow and Wednesday.

Jul 9th, 1945 Two more official evacuees returned home during the weekend, leaving one only on the first class register and one on the second class register.

Sep 10th, 1945 The school re-opened this morning after Summer Holidays. The numbers on registers Class I 20 Class II 26.

Oct 5th, 1945 Eileen Woodbridge, the last of the official evacuees on the school roll, returned to London this weekend.

Acknowledgement:
These extracts from the Cheddington School's official Log Book have been made with the kind permission of the Headteacher, Mrs K. Tamlyn, July 2010.

Appendix IV

WARTIME EXTRACTS FROM THE SCHOOL LOG AND MANAGERS' MINUTE BOOK - WARTIME CONDITIONS

[Labelled SL(School Log) and ML(Managers' Minute Book) respectively]

Sep 26th, 1939 (ML)   The Correspondent was instructed to write to the Office asking if something could be done to protect the school from an air raid – if it could not be sandbagged, something should be done to protect the windows in the corridor where Mr Jeffery said he should collect the children in the event of an Air Raid warning.

Nov 6th, 1939 (SL)   Wooden frames covered with wire netting have been fitted inside the windows of the boys' and girls' lobbies and the high window of the corridor as a precaution against flying glass fragments in the event of bomb explosion.

Dec 4th, 1939 (ML)   Two Circular letters from the Education Office were presented, one stating it was not desirable to provide dark blinds for all schools, and that where the number of evacuee children had interfered with the normal working of the school, the staff should arrange the sessions so as to give the children time to get to their homes or billets before blackout time. The putting up of wire netting guards for the windows in the corridor had been done by Mr Alcock.

Jan 15th, 1940 (ML)   A letter from the Education Office was received giving permission to darken the windows of one small classroom in schools of this sort, and that material for the same could be had from the Office. It was decided to ask for sufficient to cover the two large windows on the east side of the Infants' Room, the other side having already been done effectively by Mr Jeffery.

Mar 21st, 1940 (ML)   Arising out of the Minutes a question was asked if the dark blinds had yet been procured for the small room, and the Correspondent reported that owing to the trouble and inconvenience caused by the burst radiator and cracked stove, and the time taken in replacing these by new ones, the dark blinds had been overlooked; the Managers thought that if the blackout restrictions continued they should be obtained in readiness for next winter.

Jun 10th, 1940 (ML) (Mr Jeffery) stated that instead of closing the school for Whitsun Holiday as previously arranged, he was instructed to keep open and give lessons in the ordinary way; he did as instructed, but no children attended, or the teachers, one of which had gone away on holiday before the keep-open notice was received.

Jun 26th, 1940 (SL)   The corridor of the school has been cleared and fitted up as an air raid shelter and should provide good protection against the effects of minor explosions.

Sep 16th, 1940 (ML)   Mr Jeffery read entries from the Log from the date of the previous meeting to the present one, and stated that in view of the addition of fifty or sixty refugee, and evacuee, children which would be coming into the school this week, that a proper Air Raid Shelter should be provided, also that sufficient material for protecting all windows should be asked for; and after discussing this question at some length the Managers were unanimous in considering the lobby insufficient for protection in these dangerous times and Mr. Norris proposed, and Mr. Chandler seconded, that the Correspondent ask the Education Office to provide these precautions.
To deal with the reception and distribution of between forty and fifty more evacuees which would be coming into the Village tomorrow, Tuesday afternoon, the School would be closed then, and probably on Wednesday.

Dec 9th, 1940 (ML)   A letter from the Education Office, re the provision of an Air Raid Shelter and material for protecting windows was read by the Correspondent, saying that the Committee do not provide Shelters for schools with less than two hundred children unless they are within a two-mile radius of some definite military object, but we could have a supply of fabric for sticking on the windows.

All schools and hired buildings should be kept open during the [Christmas] holiday period for the reception and supervision of evacuated children, the teachers themselves to make their own arrangements for this purpose, the Head Teacher notifying the Office of dates and details of teachers to be on duty.

The Education Office had instructed both himself [Mr Jeffery] and Mr Spary of the Church Room School: to merge and mix the elder children into the two schools and this was being done. Some of the parents objected to this because of the greater distance from their homes and kept their children at home a few times, but things were now normal. He also reported having received the material for protecting all the windows, and that he and the teachers had done the small room but could not find time to do the large rooms, and asked if the Managers would engage someone to do this. The Correspondent was instructed to engage someone to do it.

Mar 24th, 1941 (ML) Three typed letters as received from the Education Office were read; one advocating the letting of Schools Buildings for the "Service of Youth Organisations" and one notifying the Managers of a War Allowance to be paid to all Teachers not having more than £260 per annum, to be paid as from the first of April, 1940; the other, giving advice as to Air Raid precaution and protection against fire in Schools:- arising from this the Correspondent was requested to ask for one Stirrup Pump, as this was one of the things the School had not got.

Sep 15th, 1941 (ML) Another letter from the Office was read giving authority for the Children to be taken out, under proper supervision, for the purpose of gathering blackberries to assist the food campaign; on the understanding that no single child be allowed to go on more than three afternoons during the fruit season.

Oct 15th, 1941 (SL) A consignment of food and equipment for use if and when the school is needed as an Emergency Feeding and Rest Centre was delivered by the police this morning at 10 a.m.

11 a.m. Two representatives from the Architect's department visited the school this morning to measure up window spaces, preparatory to providing a complete "black-out" for the school.

Nov 4th, 1941 (SL) During the week-end 100 blankets have been delivered for use as required in connexion with the Emergency Rest Centre.

Dec 6th, 1941 (SL) Saturday. Headmaster is on duty at school from 2 p.m. - 6 p.m. in order to meet umpires authorised by the County Controller to inspect Emergency Rest Centres.

Dec 8th, 1941 (ML) The Correspondent was asked to make some inquiry about material for blacking out one or more of the rooms at school.

Mar 16th, 1942 (ML) Arising out of the Minutes the Correspondent reported that the material to Blackout the windows at school had arrived and that the work was to be done.

Information giving the scale of War Bonus for Teachers from January 1st 1942 was read; also a letter stating that boys over twelve years of age could be allowed to do Farm Work under certain conditions and provided the consent of their parents could be obtained.

Scholars on the Register were now sixty-one local and thirteen Evacuees.

Jun 4th, 1942 (SL) Miss Joy, Ministry of Health Inspector, called at 2 p.m. to insect and report upon arrangements made to receive refugees at this Emergency Rest Centre. She left at 3.15.

Jun 8th , 1942 (ML) The Correspondent reported that all the windows in the School had now been properly blacked out.

Jun 16th, 1942 (SL) Miss Bartaby called at the school this afternoon to get information and discuss matters relative to the Emergency Rest Centre. She called at 1.15 p.m. and left at 3 p.m.

Jul 25th, 1942 (SL) Saturday. The Emergency Rest Centre staff was called together at 9 p.m. this evening, and the Centre was prepared for a full-scale exercise in conjunction with the local Civil Defence Services.

Sep 10th, 1942 (SL) Mr Leonard, Assistant Education Secretary and Revd. W T Rees called this afternoon to make enquiries regarding Emergency Rest Centre.

Mar 8th, 1944 (ML) A Circular letter [was presented to the meeting] giving the revised scale of War Allowance for Men Teachers over 21 years of age as £52 per annum, and for Women £42.

Dec 4th, 1944 Dec 1st, 1944 (SL) All Emergency Rest Centre equipment has been removed from the school.

(ML) A Circular Letter from the Education Office was read, re "Leisure Time Provision for children between the Ages of Eleven and Fourteen", asking the Managers to give consideration to this question, and the recommendation of forming youth clubs for this purpose. This the Managers did, and asked the Correspondent to reply:- that while they fully agreed as to the necessity of such clubs, under present conditions they could not see at the moment how any particular organization of this sort could be set going here, but hoped, after the War something could be done.

Dec 10th, 1945 (ML) The dark curtains supplied to the school could be kept up if needed, or taken down and made into shorts for physical training.

Acknowledgement:
These extracts from the Cheddington School's official Log Book and Minute Book have been made with the kind permission of the Headteacher, Mrs K. Tamlyn, July 2010.

Appendix V

THE BADMINTON CLUB DURING THE WAR YEARS

[Cheddington Badminton Club was formed on the 25th October 1937, and the logs of meetings since then are still in the possession of the Club. Permission has been given by members of the current committee to the History Society for their publication of Second World War memories. This has been particularly valuable in giving us a list of those who served in the forces at home and abroad during the way years. This is the only source of which we are aware that could give us such a list. Jose Cockrem has helped to give many of the first names where we had only initials.]

In **September 1939** the committee met to set the subscription for the season at 2/6d, or 3d per evening. The following month it was agreed to organise a monthly dance and profits were to go to the Red Cross Fund. Knitted garments for the troops were also to be made. Profits from these activities for the first three dances were £2 13s 3½d, £2 6s 4½d and £1 18s 2½d.

"On **22nd April 1940** Mr Gower suggested that something should be done for local boys who were serving in the forces. This was unanimously approved. Since £3 7s 1½d had been spent on wool and comforts, a balance of £8 5s 4½d was left, to be divided between the Red X and Soldier's Comforts funds. It was agreed that 10/- should be sent to all boys from the village who were serving & the remainder should be given to Red X funds.
It was decided that a receipt and stamped addressed envelope should be sent with each and that a personal letter should be sent to each one (serving in the forces). A further donation of £2 should be sent to Mrs Stoddart for the local Red Cross Fund."

On **9th September 1940** it was recorded that "the Secretary reported that 10/- had been sent to the following boys who were serving with the forces:- E Lawman, A Bonham, L Howkins, S Hurley, S Middleton, F Hing, E Hind, J Smith, R How, E Kingham, H Bonham,

G Bishop. All the boys had acknowledged the receipt of the money and personal letters had been received from all except one."

On **30th December 1940** the committee "agreed that a Military Whist Drive and Dance should be held on New Year's Eve, the proceeds to be given to the local Spitfire fund together with £3 3s 0d from the previous dance." Everyone was agreeable to having a Badminton Club Party and the date suggested was Friday 24th January and the time was fixed as 8 p.m. until after one o'clock. Visitor's cards were to be typed and one given to each member of the Club " who could invite one friend of the opposite sex and the committee could invite anyone else who would help to make the evening a success."

On **15th January 1941** it was reported that £6 6s 0d had sent to the Spitfire Fund.

6th October 1943 and it was suggested that "the Club should continue to do knitting for the forces - the Merchant Navy being thought the most worthy cause." (Six pounds was later sent). A week later and "it was agreed that the Whist Drive to be held on November 7th should be a Partner Drive and that National Savings Stamps should be given for prizes: 2 First Prizes of 5/-, 2nd Prizes 2/6, Booby Prize 1/-."

A General Meeting of the Club was arranged for Monday **9th February 1942** to decide on the allocation of the money collected for the local boys in the Forces. A total of £20 15s 3d has been collected . There is a list of 40 names of those serving in H M Forces, now including three women. [All these names are included in the overall list on the Inside Back Cover.]

On **March 2nd 1942** it was reported that " the Dance held on Feb 25th with the object of giving a supper to the Searchlight Battery and Pioneer Corps was a failure financially - but owing to the kindness of the Rector in not charging for the use of the Church Room the Club was not out of pocket."

At the Committee Meeting of **April 5th 1943** "the treasurer reported that a total profit of £17 11s 2½d had been made on the Whist Drives and Dances - £16 1s 6½d for the Local Lads Fund and £1 9s 8d for

Badminton Funds. It was unanimously agreed that a 5/- postal order should be given to each of the following members of the forces:" Fifty eight names are then given - these are included in the overall list. Now five women are named, in the Land Army and in other capacities. It was decided that wherever possible, the postal order should be delivered to the homes of the people concerned and a receipt obtained.

On **26th June 1944** it was reported that "the series of social functions held during the season had resulted in a profit of £26 8s 6½d. It was unanimously agreed that a sum of 10/- should be sent to each of the boys and girls from the village who were serving in any of H M Forces. It was found that there were 58 such people, and it was decided that the extra money required should be taken from Club funds."

On **May 2nd 1945** it was agreed that a sum of 10/- should be given to each of the boys and girls from the village who are serving in any of H M Forces. There were now 60 names - again, they are included in the overall list given in this book.

On **June 4th 1945** they outlined the rules for this distribution as a query had been received. Those eligible were: a) Permanent residents of the village (i.e. those who intend to continue their residence after the war); b) Permanent residents of Horton; c) Village boys and girls whose homes are in Cheddington or Horton; d) All ex-Badminton Club members.

August 23rd 1945 - "Miss D Sayell reported that at the request of the committee she had booked the Church Room for the first Tuesday of each of the four following months for a series of military whist drives and dances. The proceeds of these are to form the Club's main effort for the Welcome Home Fund".

On **October 5th 1945** a letter was read from the Welcome Home Committee thanking the Club for its help during Welcome Home Week. On December 10th the final total was given for the Military Whist Dance series of £21 19s 1d and it was agreed to make this up to £22 for the Welcome Home Committee.

Acknowledgements

Cheddington History Society wishes to thank all those who have given us their memories and permission to use them for this book. Many people have lent us photographs to include and we are grateful to them. Family photos have been lent to us for scanning by those whose memories are linked with them. Where these are included with the memories contributed they are not acknowledged separately but we are just as grateful! In some cases the Society has had some photographs in its archives and we do not know their provenance. If we have failed to give credit, or to acquire permission for any material, please advise us and we will amend for future editions.

We thank the Cheddington History Society Committee members for their full support.

There are others we need to thank by name. Marlene Lee, the Society's Archivist, started the ball rolling with an exhibition to celebrate VE Day in 2005. Visitors were invited to give their memories of that day. And then, like Topsy, it just growed ...

Meg Grant worked hard on our cover, giving us one that stands out from the crowd. The Old Swan was based on a 1939 photograph and a 1942 painting by C F Pashley, both of which were loaned by Neil Castle. Neil lived there during the Second World War. Behram Kapadia has given us help with getting this ready for publication. Jakki Crane, Roger Fulton, Chris and Cath Pennicott have helped us with proof reading and checking the index. We also thank Tiffany Richards and Deborah Hale who have lent us their expertise with the form of the book.

Pat Carty has let us use a number of illustrations from his book 'Secret Squadrons of the Eighth', a scholarly study of the wartime activities on Cheddington Airfield. We thank him and also the Cheddington (STN 113) Association for the illustrations on pages 8 (top), 11 (lower), 86 and both on page 93. We thank Arthur Reeve for the plan of the airfield superimposed on the land of Church Farm, Marsworth (page 8). Chas Jellis has kindly given us permission for the photos on pages 11 (top), and both on page 12. Bill Shand Kydd has let us use the photo of his brother John (page 38). We acknowledge the work on the photographs and the cover pages by John T Smith.

In addition these agencies have given us permission to use their images: the photo of the evacuee children at Wing (page 19) is from the Buckinghamshire Museum collections, the photo of the bombing in Scotland Street, Liverpool (page 32) is from the Liverpool Records Office, Liverpool Libraries, and the photo of the German bombers over East London (page 43) is from the Imperial War Museum archive.

The Leighton Buzzard Observer has allowed us to use a number of reports from the war years. Mrs Kathryn Tamlyn, Headteacher of Cheddington Combined School, has made available the School Log Book and the Managers' Minutes Book so that we could use some of their words to add much detail of the village's happenings. The Committee of the Badminton Club has lent us their Log Book for some extracts, and in particular, from the lists of those members in uniform to whom they sent postal orders, we have been able to compile a list of those who served. This is included on the Inside Back Cover. We are grateful to all for this help.

The Society is grateful to Cheddington Parish Council for their grant towards the cost of publication, and to County Councillor Avril Davies and the Buckinghamshire County Council Community Leaders' Fund for its grant.

As always, the responsibility for errors is ours. Please let us know where we have blundered - it has been a first effort, albeit a rather large one.

Lastly, we recognise the support given to the four people who have worked on this book by their partners Alan, Roger, Linda and Michael. Thanks!

INDEX